Baseball's Untold History:
The World Series

About the Author

A native of Massachusetts and the founder of **Seamheads.com**, Michael Lynch has been a member of SABR since 2004. His first book, *Harry Frazee, Ban Johnson and the Feud That Nearly Destroyed the American League*, was published by McFarland Publishing in 2008 and was named a finalist for the 2009 Larry Ritter Award in addition to being nominated for the Seymour Medal. His second book, *It Ain't So: A Might-Have-Been History of the White Sox in 1919 and Beyond*, was released by McFarland in December 2009. His work also appeared in *Opening Fenway Park in Style: The 1912 Boston Red Sox* and *The Miracle Braves of 1914: Boston's Original Worst-to-First World Series Champions*.

Michael's first Summer Game Books title was published in April 2015, *Baseball's Untold History: The People*, Volume 1 of a four-book series. Volumes 3 and 4 are scheduled for 2016.

Appearing on the front cover, clockwise from the top: Clyde McCullogh, Rube Marquard, Mickey Lolich, Ed Summers, Bill Wambsganss, Jimmy Sheckard, Gene Tenace, Ken Boyer, Jesse Haines, and center, the 1929 Philadelphia Athletics.

Baseball's Untold History: The World Series

By Michael Lynch

SUMMER
GAME
BOOKS

Portions of this book were published previously online at Seamheads.com.

ISBN: 978-1-938545-58-0 (print)
ISBN: 978-1-938545-59-7 (ebook)

For information about permissions, bulk purchases,
or additional distribution, write to
Summer Game Books
P. O. Box 818
South Orange, NJ 07079

or contact the publisher at
www.summergamebooks.com

Baseball's Untold History Series
by
Michael Lynch

Contents

Part III: 1960 - Present

Bill Wambganss executes the only triple play in World Series history, by himself.

Introduction

Welcome to Volume 2 of *Baseball's Untold History*. Volume 1, *Baseball's Untold History: The People*, focused on characters of the game that I found interesting for one reason or another—pitcher Don Wilson, who died under mysterious circumstances; Art "The Great" Shires, who began his career with four hits against Hall of Fame hurler Red Ruffing, boxed to a 5-2 record, wrestled, and was friends with notorious gangster Al Capone; and "Shufflin' Phil" Douglas, who was kidnapped on Giants manager John McGraw's orders, taken to a hospital against his will, and forced to undergo excruciating treatment for his alcoholism.

Keeping with that theme, although with much less tragedy, Volume 2 focuses on interesting characters and events that took place during the World Series. In the following pages you'll learn about:

- The 16-game winner who couldn't help his team win the World Series because he was in an insane asylum.
- The pitcher who lost a ground ball in the sun. Or did he?
- One of the most historic but overlooked Fall Classics of all-time.

- The worst performance by a pitching rotation in World Series history, and it's not even close.
- The hurler who posted a sub-1.00 ERA but failed to record a win in two starts.
- The player who went 2 for 11 in career Fall Classic steal attempts.
- A player who was arrested for scalping World Series tickets.
- The Ultimate Seven-Game Fall Classic, comprised of some of the best and/or most interesting games in World Series history. It features walk-off home runs, epic pitchers' duels, an unlikely hero, an historic comeback, and a late-inning replacement who was so high he almost misplayed an easy fly ball.

In addition to a focus on exceptional yet lesser-known post-season performances and profiles, I have also compiled some fun All-Time World Series lists: The book begins with a collection of the most unlikely heroes of the Fall Classic, which is counterbalanced later with a list of the MVPs who most exemplified "LVPs." Some of the names on both lists are sure to surprise you. And for the statistically inclined is a piece describing the oddest stat lines ever posted in the Fall Classic.

Another feature of the book – one that was a great deal of fun to research and write – is The Ultimate Fall Classic. The list is based on personal opinion, fond memories, and in some cases, moments that have stood and will continue to stand the test of time. Rather than just identify my seven favorite World Series games, however, I separated them by game and came up with my choice for the best Game One, Two, Three, Four, Five, Six, and Seven in the 113-year history of the World Series. The result is a collection of great games with great back stories, which put together make a fantastic and historic Fall Classic.

It was a difficult decision and many amazing moments were left on the cutting room floor, including the Mets' improbable come-back in Game Six of the 1986 World Series on three straight two-out singles, a wild pitch, and Bill Buckner's infamous gaffe that allowed Ray Knight to score the winning run in a 6-5 victory that staved off elimination and gave the Amazin's new life. You also won't find any games from epic Series like the 1912 clash between the Boston Red Sox and New York Giants, 1924 between the Giants and Washington Senators, or 2001 between the New York Yankees and Arizona Diamondbacks.

But six different decades are represented and highlights include four walk-off wins, seven masterful pitching performances, includ-ing by those who lost, unexpected heroes and superstars who wilted under the pressure.

No World Series book would be complete without tales of Babe Ruth, Mickey Mantle, Don Newcombe, and Mickey Lolich, and this one is no exception, but for reasons you probably won't expect. And that's the point. By the time you reach the last page, I all but guarantee you'll learn something about World Series history that you never knew.

Enjoy!

PART I:

1903 - 1929

Have We Met? The Unlikeliest World Series Heroes

The World Series is replete with heroics from the likes of Babe Ruth, Christy Mathewson, Reggie Jackson, and Randy Johnson. But every once in a while someone totally unexpected steps up and leads their team to a World Series victory. Here are nine who did just that.

George Rohe (1906) — "Whitey" Rohe was a light-hitting infielder with the Chicago White Sox who split time at third base in 1906 with even lighter-hitting Lee Tannehill, who batted a major league worst .183. Rohe's .258 average actually ranked third on the "Hitless Wonders," but he slugged only .289, which was anemic even by White Sox standards.

As a team, the White Sox hit only seven home runs and finished last in the American League in hitting, slugging, and OPS. But they also boasted a fantastic pitching staff that held opponents to a league-best 2.99 runs per game and posted a 2.13 ERA, and the Sox bested the New York Highlanders (Yankees) by three games to win the AL pennant.

Still, the cross-town Cubs were expected to easily beat the White Sox in the World Series after winning a record 116 games against only 36 losses. They had the National League's best offense, averaging 4.54 runs per game in a circuit that averaged 3.57, and they

Light-hitting infielder George Rohe led all regulars in batting and slugging, and helped the Chicago White Sox beat the heavily-favored Cubs in the 1906 World Series.

held opponents to 2.47 runs per game while posting a ridiculous 1.75 ERA, the second lowest mark in modern day history.

In Game One, Rohe tripled and scored the first run, and Nick Altrock outdueled Mordecai "Three Finger" Brown in the White Sox's 2-1 victory. Ed Reulbach almost held the White Sox hitless in Game Two, tossing six innings of no-hit ball before Jiggs Donohue reached him for a single in the seventh. Rohe reached base twice on a walk and hit by pitch in Reulbach's one-hit 7-1 gem. The Cubs' Jack Pfiester went toe-to-toe with Ed Walsh for five scoreless innings in Game Three before loading the bags in the sixth and surrendering a bases-clearing triple to Rohe, who drove in all three runs in a 3-0 win.

Brown exacted revenge on Altrock with a two-hit shutout in Game Four, and Rohe went 0 for 3, but he reached base four times in Game Five, smacked a double, and drove in a run in the Sox's 8-6 win. With his team up three games to two and on the verge of an epic upset, Rohe helped the White Sox win the Series by going 2 for 5 in Game Six with a stolen base and a run scored.

Whitey led all batters in average, on-base percentage, and slugging, and was the only player to post an OPS north of 1.000. And after stealing only eight bases in 77 regular season games, he pilfered two in six World Series games. Only Cubs shortstop Joe Tinker had more. Thanks to his fantastic performance he was given the starting third base job in 1907 at Charles Comiskey's insistence and he rewarded "The Old Roman" by being terrible, which earned him a one-way ticket out of the big leagues for good.

Hank Gowdy (1914) — Prior to 1914 Gowdy received very little playing time, amassing only 216 at-bats in 87 games from 1910-1913. Originally a first baseman, he batted .312 with 11 home runs for Dallas of the Texas League in 1910 and earned a cup of coffee with the New York Giants, who already boasted 21-year-old Fred Merkle at first. Merkle was one of John McGraw's best players and Gowdy had little chance to crack the lineup, so McGraw suggested that Gowdy try catching.

He was traded to the Boston Braves in 1911[1] and after stops and starts in which he showed promise, Gowdy was named Boston's starting catcher in 1914. On paper his slash line of .243/.337/.347 doesn't look all that impressive, but his .684 OPS was better than league average and almost 50 points better than the average catcher. He also threw out 52% of would-be base stealers, eight points better than league average.

Still, I.E. Sanborn of the *Chicago Tribune* wrote that the Philadelphia Athletics had a "decided advantage" behind the plate with World Series veteran Wally Schang sporting the wire mask[2]. Unlike Gowdy, the 24-year-old A's backstop was a star from the beginning, finishing eighth in MVP voting as a rookie in 1913, then starring against the Giants in the World Series, batting

.357 and driving home seven runs in four games to lead his club to victory.

But it was Gowdy who stole the show in the 1914 World Series, at least at the plate. The Braves' catcher went 3 for 3 in Game One with a double, a triple, two runs, an RBI, a walk, and a stolen base. He went 0 for 2 against legendary southpaw Eddie Plank in the second tilt, but walked twice in a 1-0 Braves win; rapped out three more hits—two doubles and a homer—against Chief Bender in Game Three; and walked in three trips to the plate in Game Four to help the Braves complete an improbable sweep.

He finished the Series with a slash line of .545/.688/1.273 and an OPS of 1.960. Five of his six hits went for extra bases and he drew five walks against only one strikeout. And, for good measure, he threw out Rube Oldring on a steal attempt and picked Jimmy Walsh off second base in Boston's Game Four win. His OPS in the 1914 Fall Classic still ranks sixth all-time among players with at least 10 plate appearances.

Tommy Thevenow (1926) — Once upon a time if you were a middle infielder or catcher on a pennant-winning team, you were all but guaranteed a ton of MVP support. Take St. Louis Cardinals shortstop Tommy Thevenow, for example. In 1926 the 22-year-old enjoyed his first full season and was absolutely horrible at the plate, batting .256/.294/.311 for an OPS+ of 59, 41% worse than league average.

To put that into perspective, no other Cards hitter had an OPS+ below 100, and all but Taylor Douthit were at 112 or above. That said, Thevenow was the best defensive shortstop in all of baseball and MVP voters absolutely loved pennant-winning infielders back then, so he finished fourth on the ballot behind teammate Bob O'Farrell (did I mention they also loved pennant-winning catchers?), Cincinnati second baseman Hughie Critz, and Pirates pitcher Rey Kremer.

Prior to the World Series against the Yankees, Thevenow experienced a "power" surge and hit home runs on September 17 and 22, albeit both were of the inside-the-park variety. Still, he'd gone almost 800 career at-bats before he finally rounded the bases on his own volition, and he did it twice in five days.

He went 0 for 2 in Game One of the 1926 Fall Classic, but successfully sacrificed O'Farrell to second with no outs in the seventh and the Yankees leading 2-1 only to see Herb Pennock work out of the jam and hold on for the win. He went 3 for 4 in Game Two with another inside-the-park home run made possible when Babe Ruth made an attempt to catch the ball, then couldn't locate it while Thevenow raced around the bases, scored twice, and drove in a run in St. Louis' 6-2 victory.

He failed to record a hit in Game Three but scored a run in a 4-0 win; he went 2 for 4 with a double, a run, and an RBI in a Game Four loss; swatted another hit in Game Five; reached base three times and scored a run in Game Six; and went 2 for 3 with two RBIs in the Cards' 3-2 win in a seventh game that ended when Ruth was caught stealing with slugger Bob Meusel at the plate.

Thevenow batted .417 and scored five runs in seven games, prompting Rogers Hornsby to call him "the best shortstop in baseball."[3] His home run against Sad Sam Jones in Game Two would be the last of his career. He played another 12 years without hitting a four-bagger and set a record that still stands by going 3,347 at-bats without a homer.

Al Weis (1969) — Weis was a light-hitting middle infielder who signed a free agent deal with the Chicago White Sox in 1959, then proceeded to hit .219 in a 10-year major league career that began in 1962. After batting .239 with only three home runs from 1962-1967, Weis was traded to the New York Mets along with Tommie Agee, and they'd both play pivotal roles in the 1969 World Series.

In 1968 the entire National League batted only .243, but Weis was particularly bad, weighing in with a .172 mark in 274 at-bats. Weis' hitting continued to be anemic in 1969—he hit only .215 in 103 games—but he actually tied career bests in doubles, homers, and RBIs, albeit with paltry totals that few would brag about.

After getting only one at-bat in the NLCS against the Atlanta Braves, Weis went crazy against the Baltimore Orioles in the World Series. In Game One he drew two walks against eventual American League Cy Young Award winner Mike Cuellar, and drove in the Mets' only run with a seventh-inning sacrifice fly. In Game Two he helped New York tie the Series at a game apiece by going 2 for 3 with a walk and the game-winning RBI.

He went 2 for 3 with a walk in Game Four, then capped off the Mets' miraculous Series win with a home run off 20-game winner Dave McNally in the seventh inning of Game Five to help his team to a 5-3 win. The slender switch hitter hit only seven home runs in his major league career and all of them were in road parks until his Game Five blast at Shea Stadium. Weis batted .455 with an on-base percentage of .563 and only World Series MVP Donn Clendenon drove in more runs than the "Mighty Mite."

Gene Tenace (1972) — In 1972 the 25-year-old Tenace was backing up 26-year-old catcher Dave Duncan, as he had the previous season when Duncan became Oakland's starter. Duncan had belted 46 homers for Class A Modesto in 1966 when he was just 20 and had a reputation as a "fine young defensive backstop."[4] As a major leaguer he had above average home run totals for a catcher and belted a career-high 19 in 1972, but was below average in almost every other category and batted only .217 from 1964-'72.

Tenace, on the other hand, posted three straight very good seasons in the minors and was already displaying excellent strike zone judgment as a 20-year-old. After a cup of coffee with the A's in

A's catcher Gene Tenace hit five home runs in 82 regular season games in 1972, then hit four in the first five games of the '72 Fall Classic.

1969, Tenace was very good as their third-string catcher, posting a slash line of .305/.430/.562 and hitting seven homers in 31 games. He was very good again in '71 before taking a step backwards in '72 when he batted only .225/.307/.339, but he became Oakland's primary starting catcher in September after Duncan batted only .163 in August and September.

Tenace was terrible at the plate in the ALCS against the Tigers, going hitless in the first four games before driving in what would prove to be the winning run with a single in Game Five. Despite his .059/.200/.059 showing, the A's won and advanced to the World Series against the Reds. And that's when Tenace took center stage.

He single-handedly beat Cincinnati in Game One and established a new record in the process when he homered in his first two World

Series at-bats. Tenace drove in all three Oakland runs in a 3-2 win, including the tie-breaker in the fifth with a solo homer off Gary Nolan. He went hitless in Game Two, but the A's squeaked out a 2-1 win behind the pitching of Catfish Hunter and Rollie Fingers; then he went 0 for 3 in a 1-0 Game Three loss.

At that point he was only 2 for 10, but with two homers, three RBIs, and two runs scored. He erupted again in Game Four and went 2 for 4 with another home run, two runs, and an RBI in Oakland's 3-2 victory. The Reds took Game Five, 5-4, but it wasn't Tenace's fault as he went 1 for 2 with a three-run homer, and two walks. He rapped out a single in a Game Six loss, then capped off his brilliant series with two more hits, including a double in a Game Seven win, in which he knocked in two of the A's Three runs.

Tenace's four home runs tied a World Series record that has since been broken and he drove in nine of his team's 16 runs. Those would be the only home runs he'd hit in 42 postseason games.

Brian Doyle (1978) — Doyle, whose older brother Denny may be most known for trying to score the winning run for the Red Sox in the bottom of the ninth inning of Game Six of the 1975 World Series, only to be thrown out at the plate by Reds left fielder George Foster, was drafted by the Texas Rangers in the fourth round of the 1972 amateur draft right out of Caverna High School in Horse Cave, Kentucky.

His professional career got off to a promising start at age 17 when he posted a .390 on-base percentage and went 16 for 20 in stolen base attempts in Single A. But he steadily regressed at the plate and couldn't find any consistency in the field. Despite establishing then-career bests in almost every offensive category in 1976, including batting (.301) and slugging (.382), the 22-year-old infielder was traded to the Yankees in February 1977.

He was mostly terrible for Syracuse in 1977 before rebounding in 1978 with Tacoma, albeit in a role limited by the presence of 21-year-old prospect Damaso Garcia. Doyle made his major league debut on April 30, 1978 and played sparingly, which wasn't surprising considering he batted .192/.192/.192 with 10 singles in 52 at-bats. With the Yankees battling the Red Sox down to the wire, one of their worst nightmares came true—regular second baseman Willie Randolph pulled his left hamstring on September 29 with only two games left on the schedule.

Randolph was having a career year and easily led the Yankees in on-base percentage. In his absence, Doyle and Fred "Chicken" Stanley went a combined 0 for 9 with a walk in the final three games of the season, including a one-game playoff against the Red Sox to determine who would go to the playoffs. The Yankees beat Boston and Doyle acquitted himself well in the ALCS against the Royals, hitting .286 with a walk and an RBI in three games. In fact, his .375 on-base average wasn't much lower than Randolph's regular season mark.

Prior to driving in Graig Nettles with a fifth-inning single in Game One, Doyle had never knocked in a run in a major league game. The Yankees beat the Royals in four games and faced the Los Angeles Dodgers in the World Series, and that's when Doyle caught lightening in a bottle. Well...eventually.

After watching most of Game One from the dugout, he went 1 for 3 in Game Two and 0 for 4 in Game Three, and landed on the bench again for Game Four. With the Series tied at two games apiece, Doyle's bat woke up in Game Five and he went 3 for 5 with two runs scored in a 12-2 Yankees rout. Then he went 3 for 4 with a double, two runs, and two RBIs to help lead New York to a 7-2 win and yet another World Series victory.

The double, off Hall of Famer Don Sutton no less, was his first ever major league extra-base hit. Doyle's .438 average led the Yanks, and his .938 OPS was third behind only Reggie Jackson and Paul Blair. He might be the unlikeliest World Series hero in history; he spent only three more years in the majors and finished with a career batting average of .161 in 199 at-bats.

Dane Iorg (1982/1985) — Iorg was a utility man who played multiple positions, and even pitched twice, and he enjoyed some pretty good seasons at the plate in a platoon role, batting .304 from 1979-1982 with a high of .327 for the St. Louis Cardinals in 1981. In 1982, Iorg hit .294 with a career-best .352 on-base percentage while splitting time between the outfield and first base, and helped the Cardinals win the National League pennant.

With Lonnie Smith in left field, George Hendrick in right, and Keith Hernandez at first, Iorg saw no playing time in the Cards' three-game sweep over the Atlanta Braves in the NLCS. But the designated hitter rule that allowed both teams to employ a DH in even numbered years gave St. Louis and extra bat in the lineup, and Iorg stepped up in the role.

The aforementioned Gene Tenace served as the Cardinals' DH in Game One and went hitless. Iorg got the call in Game Two and went 1 for 2 before being lifted for a pinch hitter. He went 1 for 4 with a double and a run in Game Three, then rapped out two hits and drove in a run in Game Four. After sitting out Game Five and watching the Milwaukee Brewers go up three games to two after a 6-4 win, Iorg turned up the heat with a 3 for 4 effort in Game Six that included two doubles and a triple, then helped the Cardinals wrap up the Series with two more hits in Game Seven.

When all was said and done, Iorg led all hitters with a 1.412 OPS and it wasn't even close. He finished with nine hits in five games, five of which went for extra bases, and batted .529 for the Series.

By 1985, his skills had betrayed him and his career was coming to an end. He batted only .223 for the Kansas City Royals in a limited role, but came up big again in the World Series when he won Game Six against his former team with a two-run pinch-hit single in the bottom of the ninth to give the Royals a 2-1 victory. Thanks to Iorg, the Royals lived to see another day and trounced the Cardinals, 11-0, in Game Seven to cop their first championship in franchise history.

Kurt Bevacqua (1984) — Bevacqua spent 15 years in the majors, probably because he could play six different positions, albeit none very well, and was passable as a pinch hitter. His career high in at-bats was 297 in 1979 and he averaged just 141 per season. In 1984, his penultimate season, the 37-year-old batted only .200 with one homer and nine RBIs in 80 at-bats for the San Diego Padres.

In the NLCS against the Cubs, Bevacqua batted only twice and grounded into a double play. But thanks to the rules at the time, Bevacqua landed in San Diego's starting lineup as their designated hitter all throughout their series against the Detroit Tigers.

He began the Series with a 1 for 3 effort, in which he doubled off Tigers ace Jack Morris in a 3-2 loss, then led the Padres to their only victory, a 5-3 win , in which he went 3 for 4 with a go-ahead home run off Dan Petry and drove in three of his team's five runs. He singled in Game Three, doubled in Game Four, and homered again in Game Five, and scored two of San Diego's four runs.

Though the Tigers easily won the 1984 Fall Classic, when the dust settled no regular had a higher OPS than Bevacqua's 1.327, not even Alan Trammell (1.300) who was named the Series MVP. Bevacqua batted .412 and slugged .882, and did everything he could to lead his team to victory. Unfortunately the next best Padres hitter—Alan Wiggins—had an OPS of "only" .773, and San Diego's rotation was brutal.

Billy Hatcher (1990) — Hatcher spent 12 years in the major leagues and certainly had his moments, especially in 1987 when the then-Houston Astros outfielder batted .296 with 11 homers, 63 RBIs, and a career-high 53 stolen bases, which was good for third in the National League. His 106 OPS+ was also a career high and though he'd post a 102 mark in 1988, he'd never be as good as he was in those consecutive seasons.

After splitting time between the Astros and Pirates in 1989, Hatcher was traded to the Cincinnati Reds in 1990, with whom he was decent at the plate, batting .276 and stealing 30 bases, but excellent in the outfield where he committed only one error all season. The Reds edged the Dodgers and Giants to cop the NL West division title, then defeated the Pirates in the NLCS for the right to meet the powerful Oakland A's, who won their third straight pennant and were the defending champions.

Hatcher had a very good series against the Pirates, hitting .333 with a homer, two RBIs, and two runs scored, but it was against the A's that he made his mark and set a new World Series record. He set the tone in Game One against A's ace Dave Stewart when he went 3 for 3 with three runs, two doubles, an RBI, and a walk in a 7-0 Cincinnati victory. He was even better in Game Two, going 4 for 4 with two runs, two more doubles, a triple, an RBI, and a walk.

His seven consecutive hits broke the previous record of six held by Goose Goslin (1924) and Thurman Munson (1976). He grounded into a double play in his first at-bat of Game Three to break his streak, but went 2 for 5 and scored another run to help lead the Reds to their third straight win. Hatcher reached base in his first plate appearance in Game Four, but didn't get a chance to continue padding his stats as Stewart knocked him out of the game with a bruised left hand when he drilled Hatcher with a two-strike pitch.

The Reds swept the A's in four straight and Hatcher finished the Series with a .750 batting average, a record for a four-game Fall Classic.

Ed Doheny: The Paranoid Pirate

Upper Row—Kennedy, Leever, Phillippe, Beaumont, Veil, Thompson, Ritchey, Carisch.
Middle Row—Phelps, Bransfield, Leach, Clarke, Weaver, Wagner, Smith,
Lower Row—Marshall, Kruger, Sebring, Pfeister.
*Note—Doheny was sick and Winham absent when this picture was taken.

This photo of the 1903 NL champion Pittsburgh Pirates is more notable for who isn't in it than who is. The note at the bottom says "Doheny was sick...when this picture was taken." Doheny is Ed

Doheny, a southpaw who went 37-69 from 1895 to 1901 for the New York Giants before being released. The Pirates picked Doheny off the scrap heap and he rewarded them with a 38-14 mark over 2 1/2 seasons from 1901-1903.

In 1903 he was the third wheel of an excellent trio of hurlers that included Sam Leever (25-7, 2.06), Deacon Phillippe (25-9, 2.43) and Doheny (16-8, 3.19), but wasn't able to face Boston in the first modern day World Series because he was no longer with the team.

After starting the season 12-6 that year, he began exhibiting odd behavior and believed he was being followed by detectives, prompting him to leave the team and head home to Massachusetts to rest, and causing newspapers to call him "deranged."[1] Friends and family assumed he was just tired and nervous about pitching in the big leagues, so they paid no attention to his behavior.[2]

He rejoined the team after a few weeks and continued to win, but made his last start on September 7 before going home for more rest. Pirates manager Fred Clarke had been in contact with Doheny's physician, who told him Doheny "couldn't be depended upon" for the World Series. "Of course we sometime ago gave up all expectation of Doheny's helping us in the present series," Clarke told reporters, "but I had hoped he would be all right for next season."[3]

Despite being under the daily care of Dr. E.C. Conroy, Doheny's condition worsened until he finally snapped. Conroy checked in on Doheny on October 10, but was told his services were no longer needed. Conroy tried to coax Doheny into continuing his treatment, but the pitcher ordered the doctor to leave his house. When Conroy failed to comply, Doheny hit him in the face and escorted him to the sidewalk.

Police were called but it was decided that he just needed rest, so another doctor and nurse were called in to help him calm down, which they did. The next morning Doheny became violent. While his nurse, Oberlin Howarth, had his back turned Doheny struck him on the head repeatedly with a cast-iron stove leg he'd concealed in his bed. The blows opened a large gash on Howarth's head and knocked him unconscious.

Neighbors rushed to Howarth's aid only to find Doheny at his front door wielding the bloody stove leg and threatening anyone who came near him. After a one-hour stand-off with neighbors and police, Doheny was taken into custody and committed to the Danvers Lunatic Asylum.

Sadly, the hurler deteriorated to the point where he no longer recognized family and friends, including his own wife. He spent the last 13 years of his life in asylums before he died on December 29, 1916 at the Medfield State Asylum in Massachusetts. He's buried in his home state of Vermont.

The Ultimate Fall Classic: Game One

October 15, 1988—Oakland A's at Los Angeles Dodgers: The A's, led by "Bash Brothers" Jose Canseco (.307/42/124 and 40 steals) and Mark McGwire (32 HR and 99 RBIs), 21-game winner Dave Stewart, and closer Dennis Eckersley, who led the league with 45 saves, cruised to a 104-58 record and made a mockery of the AL West, finishing 13 games ahead of the second-place Minnesota Twins. Then they pounded the Red Sox in the ALCS to earn their first World Series berth since 1974.

The Dodgers were a less dominating, albeit still impressive, 94-67, and they needed seven games to dispatch the heavily favored NL East champion New York Mets in the NLCS to earn their second World Series berth of the decade. Offensively, the Dodgers weren't nearly the equal of the A's, boasting no .300 hitters or 100-RBI men, and only three players with 10 or more homers—Kirk Gibson, who led the team with 25, Mike Marshall, who belted 20, and John Shelby, who smacked 10. Like the A's, the Dodgers claimed only one 20-game winner, Orel Hershiser, who went 23-8 with a 2.26 ERA, but had two other starters—Tim Leary and Tim Belcher—who sported ERAs under 3.00, both coming in at 2.91. And the Dodgers' bullpen featured a closing tandem of Jay Howell and Alejandro Pena, who combined for 33 saves and a 1.98 ERA in almost 160 innings.

As a team, the Dodgers averaged 3.9 runs per game; the A's averaged almost five runs a game, giving them a clear advantage on offense. The entire Dodgers team hit only 99 four-baggers; Canseco, McGwire, and center fielder Dave Henderson (24) hit 98 by themselves, and the A's belted 156 as a team. The pitching seemed to favor the Dodgers, who ranked second in the NL in ERA at 2.96 and runs allowed per game at 3.4, while the A's, who also finished second in ERA and runs per game, weren't as impressive at 3.44 and 3.8, respectively.

Regardless, Oakland was a heavy favorite going into the Series and few thought the Dodgers could win. Thomas Boswell of the *Washington Post* predicted the A's would win in five.[1] Writer Phil Elderkin called the matchup a battle of the "resourceful Dodgers" vs. "Oakland's power company" and wrote something that proved prescient: "Barring the unexpected, this is a series that pits Oakland's power, pitching, and defense against the Dodgers' pitching, timely hitting, and hard-to-explain ability to overcome seemingly impossible odds."[2]

The odds became even more "seemingly impossible" when Gibson, the battered star of the Dodgers, was unable to take batting practice the day before Game One due to a sore left hamstring and a sprained medial collateral ligament in his right knee. Gibson was the statistical and spiritual leader of the club, setting the tone early in the season when he went ballistic on the first day of spring training when pitcher Jesse Orosco smeared eye black on Gibson's cap as a practical joke.[3] It was mostly because of his leadership that Gibson was eventually named NL MVP despite posting numbers that were inferior to players like Daryl Strawberry of the Mets and Will Clark of the Giants.

Instead of Gibson in left field, Lasorda went with his star's polar opposite, the affable and fun-loving Mickey Hatcher, a 10-year veteran with a .282 career batting average, but only 36 homers in more than 3,000 career at-bats. Hatcher hit .293 in 1988 with only one home run in 191 at-bats, but Lasorda penciled Hatcher into the three hole, the same spot occupied by Canseco, the first 40-40 man in baseball history and that year's runaway winner of the AL MVP award.

Lasorda was also hamstrung in the pitching department after going with Hershiser in Game Seven of the NLCS. Not wanting to run his ace out there on only two days rest, Lasorda went with rookie Tim Belcher, who went 12-6 in 27 regular season starts, then beat the Mets twice in the playoffs. A's manager Tony LaRussa had no such problem, as his ace, Dave Stewart, last threw in Game Four of the ALCS on October 9 and was well rested.

Belcher struggled early, loading the bases in the top of the first when he surrendered a single to Dave Henderson, hit Canseco with a pitch, and walked McGwire, but he coaxed catcher Terry Steinbach to fly out to end the inning without allowing a run. Stewart wasn't sharp either; he hit Steve Sax in the middle of the back with his first pitch of the game, prompting home plate umpire Doug Harvey to issue warnings to both benches, then with Hatcher at the plate and one out, he balked Sax to second.

Hatcher made Lasorda look like a genius when he deposited a Stewart offering into the left field seats for a two-run homer and gave the home crowd a show by running around the bases like his hair was on fire. "It was as if he thought they would suddenly change their minds and take it back," said Dodgers third base coach Joey Amalfitano.[4]

Stewart got out of the inning without further damage and looked to his powerful teammates to come to his rescue. They didn't disappoint. Glenn Hubbard singled, Walt Weiss struck out, and Stewart and Carney Lansford walked to load the bases. It clearly wasn't Belcher's day; he'd faced 10 batters and six had reached base via hit, walk, or hit by pitch. Lasorda had Tim Leary start warming up in the bullpen when Belcher fell behind Lansford. When Belcher fell behind Dave Henderson, southpaw Ricky Horton began warming up as well.

The rookie recovered briefly and fanned Henderson, but he still had to face Canseco with the bases juiced and two outs. Belcher fell behind again, throwing a ball to Canseco on his first pitch. Then he threw one more to Canseco's liking and the behemoth slugger lined a 400-foot shot over the center field fence for a grand slam to give Oakland a 4-2 lead. The homer proved to be Canseco's only hit of the Series in 22 plate appearances.

Belcher walked Dave Parker, drawing the ire of the home town faithful, then retired McGwire on a fielder's choice grounder to short to end the inning, but Lasorda had seen enough and yanked the rookie from the game, pinch hitting Danny Heep in the bottom of the second. Stewart had little trouble with the Dodgers in the last of the second.

Tim Leary entered the game for the Dodgers in the top of the third and ran into immediate trouble when Steinbach hit a smash that third baseman Jeff Hamilton knocked down but couldn't handle, then advanced to second on a base hit to left by Hubbard. But Leary worked out of the jam by retiring Weiss on a flyout, striking out Stewart, and coaxing Lansford to ground out. Except for a two-out walk to Hatcher, Stewart handled the Dodgers again in the third and led 4-2 going into the fourth.

Dave Henderson led off the fourth with a ground rule double into the right field corner, but got caught off second base on a Canseco grounder to Griffin at short and was tagged out. Then Parker plunked a short grounder to the right side that was fielded by Leary, who drilled Parker in the right shoulder with his throw to first. Canseco advanced all the way to third and Parker went to second on the errant throw, but Harvey called Parker out for running out of the baseline, which brought LaRussa out of the dugout for a futile argument.

Canseco was sent back to first but wasn't there long, stealing second base with McGwire at the plate. The move backfired when Lasorda ordered an intentional walk to McGwire and Leary fanned Steinbach to end the inning. Stewart and Leary traded three-up/three-downs in the bottom of the fourth and top of the fifth, respectively, but when Griffin walked to lead off the bottom of the fifth, Lasorda yanked Leary in favor of pinch hitter Tracy Woodson. But Stewart sandwiched two groundouts and a fly out around a wild pitch and the Dodgers stranded yet another runner on base.

Lasorda went to his pen again in the sixth and brought righty Brian Holton into the game. The 28-year-old enjoyed a career year, going 7-3 with a save and a microscopic 1.70 ERA in 45 appearances, and he was murder on right-handed batters. Holton wasted no time neutralizing Oakland's power, retiring Lansford, Canseco, and Henderson.

The Dodgers finally parlayed again in the bottom of the sixth courtesy of consecutive singles by Mike Marshall, John Shelby, and Mike Scioscia, which cut the score to 4-3 in favor of the A's, but Stewart survived without further damage when Hamilton grounded into an inning-ending double play. Both teams reached base again in the seventh, but both stranded runners at second and the A's clung to their slim 4-3 lead.

Lasorda summoned Alejandro Pena into the game to start the eighth. Pena was in his eighth year in the league and became a full-time reliever in 1988, posting a 1.91 ERA in 60 appearances and recording a then career-high 12 saves. He had no trouble with the A's, retiring Weiss, Stewart, and Lansford in order; Stewart returned the favor in the bottom of the frame, striking out Hatcher, popping up Marshall, and getting Shelby to fly out to Canseco in right.

Pena accepted the challenge and fanned Henderson and Canseco to start off the top of the ninth, surrendered a single to Stan Javier, who had pinch run for Parker earlier in the game, then retired

McGwire on a foul fly to right, setting up one of the most exciting finishes in baseball history.

With the A's clinging to a one-run lead, LaRussa went to his bullpen and summoned closer Dennis Eckersley into the game. Stewart was in command and had thrown only 98 pitches, but Eckersley had established himself as the best closer in the junior circuit. He had 45 saves on the year, a 2.35 ERA, and 70 strikeouts in 72 2/3 innings, but what was most impressive is that he walked only 11 batters all year, and two of those were intentional. He was also equally effective against righties and lefties, holding the former to a .197 average and two homers in 148 plate appearances, and the latter to a .198 average and three homers in 131 plate appearances.

Eckersley was coming off a masterful performance, in which he saved all four A's victories over the Red Sox in the ALCS, allowing only one hit in six innings, while fanning five, and was named MVP of the series. He showed the Dodgers how valuable he was when he retired Scioscia and Hamilton on five pitches, popping Scioscia up to Weiss and whiffing Hamilton on three straight offerings. With Griffin due up and Los Angeles down to their last out, Lasorda called on lefty swinger Mike Davis to pinch hit.

Davis batted only .196 with two homers and 17 RBIs in 108 games, and he wasn't much better against righties, hitting only .203, although with both homers and 10 of his 17 ribbies. With the quick-working Eckersley on the mound, Lasorda told Davis to disrupt his timing by stepping out of the box. Then Lasorda deked the A's by having right-handed hitting utility infielder Dave Anderson swing a bat in the on-deck circle. Anderson was a .232 career hitter with 12 home runs in almost 1,500 career at-bats, and Lasorda figured that when Eckersley saw Anderson getting ready to hit, he'd pitch around Davis to get to the light-hitting righty.

Davis fouled off Eckersley's first offering, then did as instructed, frequently stepping out of the box and throwing off Eckersley's timing. "The guy's hitting a buck ninety—what the hell's he doing calling time?" the closer asked later. Then Eck threw four straight balls and walked him. "I wasn't pitching around him," Eckersley insisted. "Not at all. I was going right at him."[5]

He had faced 302 batters in the regular season, ALCS, and World Series to that point and had walked only 11 of them. Davis was the 12th and it would come back to haunt Eckersley and the A's.

Meanwhile, unbeknown to most, Kirk Gibson began limbering up in the clubhouse at the start of the inning. But when Davis came on to pinch hit for Griffin and Anderson took his spot in the on-deck circle, it looked like Gibson would remain firmly planted on the Dodgers' bench. Once Davis reached base, though, Anderson gave way to Gibson, who received a thunderous ovation from the crowd as he limped his way to the plate.

The slugger had been pacing back and forth between the clubhouse and the trainer's room, icing his knee, which had already been injected with cortisone, and taking swings in the batting cage, and he was ready.

Eckersley came right after Gibson with a fastball, which the slugger fouled off, then hobbled out of the box. The closer would later explain that due to Gibson's condition, he wanted to go with nothing but fastballs away to try to coax him to hit a weak fly ball to left. With the crowd on its feet imploring their hero to perform a miracle, Gibson stepped back into the box and awaited Eck's next offering. The pitcher alternated between throwing to first to keep Davis close and throwing to the plate, and when he came home, Gibson fouled that off too and the count went to 0-2.

A couple more tosses to first preceded Eckersley's next pitch, which Gibson hit weakly down the first base line, then feebly limped towards first before the ball rolled foul. "They were such bad swings, you could feel Gibson's pain from the upper deck," wrote Jayson Stark of the *Philadelphia Inquirer.* "You wondered what he was even doing out there."[6]

Eckersley's next pitch was a ball, but the game almost ended when catcher Ron Hassey, who'd entered the game in the bottom of the ninth for defensive purposes, threw a bullet to first that almost caught Davis before he scrambled back safely to the bag.

On Eckersley's next pitch, Davis took off for second, but Gibson fouled it away. Then Eck came back with a high fastball that Gibson took for ball two. Eckersley threw over to first one more time, then came to the plate. Gibson took the pitch for ball three and Davis took second base without a throw. Now, with a runner in scoring position, Gibson slightly adjusted his approach.

With first base open, LaRussa chose to pitch to Gibson rather than have Eckersley walk him and face the on-deck batter, Steve Sax. "I knew they had a tough hitter in the on-deck circle," LaRussa said. "And I figured the best thing to do was have Dennis go right at [Gibson]."[7] Whether LaRussa knew it or not, Sax had been money with runners in scoring position that year, batting .350, and was especially dangerous with two outs, batting .419 with a .520 on-base percentage. Besides, the A's skipper wasn't about to put the winning run on base.

After feeding Gibson a steady diet of fastballs, Hassey called for a slider. "We had been throwing him all those fastballs, and I felt like we could freeze him with the breaking ball," the catcher later explained.[8] Eckersley wanted to keep throwing smoke, but didn't shake off his catcher and decided to throw the nastiest slider he could. But it got too much of the plate.

Here's Jack Buck's call:

"Gibson swings, and a fly ball to deep right field! This is gonna be a home run! Unbelievable! A home run for Gibson! And the Dodgers have won the game, 5 to 4; I don't believe what I just saw! I don't believe what I just saw!"

"Gibson, with one blow, restored the magic usually reserved for such things as Disneyland and Alice in Wonderland," wrote Larry Whiteside. "Who would have thought that a man, hobbled by injuries and unable to run, would be able to come through in the clutch against Oakland's Dennis Eckersley."[9]

"It was a great moment," Gibson said after the game. "And I felt fortunate to be there and be a part of it. This was a classic."[10]

Indeed it was.

Bill Abstein: Floundering at First Base

After suffering with four mostly terrible first basemen in 1908, the Pittsburgh Pirates acquired "Big Bill" Abstein from Providence of the Eastern League in the hope he'd improve the initial station in 1909. Abstein, a native of St. Louis, showed promise as a 21-year-old when he batted .310 with 12 homers for Houston in 1904, then hit .311 for Shreveport in 1906.

He batted only .275 with 12 homers from 1907-1908, but earned a spot in the majors after Pittsburgh's first basemen hit only .225 with one home run in 599 at-bats. The *Boston Globe* was less than impressed with Abstein, though, and predicted an early demise. "Those who noted the awful slump in Abstein's work at first base for the Providence club last season can see the young man's early finish trying to hold down the base for the Pittsburg club."[1]

"Big Bill" played 137 games and manned first base in 135 of them. He was among the worst first basemen in the league, both offensively and defensively, but finished third on the Pirates in RBIs with 70. He also finished second in strikeouts with 59 and only Reds first baseman Dick Hoblitzell finished with more errors at first base in the senior circuit than Abstein's 27. Manager Fred Clarke told Pirates owner Barney Dreyfuss as early as June that the team would need a new first baseman in 1910 because Abstein was "mixing up the plays."[2]

Regardless, the Pirates won 110 games, establishing themselves as one of the greatest teams in major league history, and met the American League champion Detroit Tigers in a World Series that pitted 22-year-old superstar Ty Cobb against 35-year-old legend Honus Wagner. Cobb was coming off a triple crown year in which he batted .377 with nine home runs and 107 runs batted in; Wagner won his seventh batting title at .339 and won his fourth RBI crown with 100.

Game One went to the Pirates, 4-1, behind rookie hurler Babe Adams. Abstein went 0 for 3 with a run, an RBI, a walk, and a strikeout, and he was picked off first by George Mullin. The Tigers tied the series with a convincing 7-2 win in Game Two, in which Abstein went 1 for 4 with three strikeouts and an error. Abstein's bat woke up in Games Three and Four when he went 3 for 8 with a double and a run, but he committed four errors and his pair of miscues in Game Three almost cost the Pirates the game.

Behind 6-0 going into the seventh inning, the Tigers mounted a comeback and scored four runs, three of which were unearned after Abstein failed to handle a throw from Dots Miller. The Pirates doubled their lead to 8-4 in the top of the ninth, but the Tigers plated two more in the bottom half on two more unearned runs after Abstein dropped a throw from Wagner that would have been the second out of the inning. Instead Detroit parlayed a single, a Cobb double and a groundout into two runs before Pittsburgh got out of the inning and held on for the 8-6 win.

His two errors in Game Four had nothing to do with the Tigers' 5-0 victory—he muffed a first-inning pickoff of Cobb that allowed the Tiger to reach second, and fumbled a grounder in the third— but they didn't endear him to his teammates who were becoming frustrated with his sloppy play and let him know about it.[3] The *St. Louis Post-Dispatch* reported that veteran center fielder Tommy Leach couldn't stand Abstein, and the first baseman was so fearful of making errors that he was taking throws on his knees so the ball wouldn't get past him.[4] There was also a rumored "bitter fight" between Abstein and pitcher Vic Willis during the Series.[5]

Abstein didn't make another fielding error for the rest of the series, but an alleged base running error in Game Six put him in the spotlight again and all but guaranteed his ticket out of town. With the Tigers up 5-3 going into the top of the ninth at Detroit's Bennett Park, the Pirates rallied and scored a run to pull to within one at 5-4.

Miller and Abstein singled off George Mullin to put runners at first and second with nobody out. Chief Wilson laid down a bunt in front of the plate and Tigers catcher Boss Schmidt fielded it and fired to first, but Wilson and first baseman Tom Jones collided on the play and in the confusion Miller scored and Abstein scampered to third.

But the *St. Louis Post-Dispatch* reported that Abstein should have scored as well and tied the game. "When Tom Jones was knocked senseless at first base Abstein could have scored with ease," opined the paper. "Abstein went from first to third, then

Pirates first baseman Bill Abstein committed five errors in the 1909 World Series and established a record among Fall Classic first sackers that still stands.

stopped there and gazed in wonder at poor Tom stretched on the ground."[6] The *Washington Post* reported that Jones was so badly hurt on the play that he needed to be carried off the field.[7]

Then the Pirates first sacker made another "bone-head" play when he hesitated, then attempted to score on a grounder to first and was thrown out at the plate by four feet.[8] Rumors surfaced that a frustrated Abstein addressed his teammates in a meeting the day before Game Seven and told them he was through with the team as soon as the World Series was over.[9] Apparently he didn't realize he was already on his way out the door.

"Fred Clarke announced that he had purchased four first basemen to be tried out with the Pirates next spring," announced the Post-Dispatch after Game Six.[10] The ink was barely dry but the writing was on the wall.

The Pirates easily won Game Seven, 8-0, behind Babe Adams who won his third game of the Series. Abstein went 1 for 4 with a run, a stolen base, and a strikeout, and finished the Series with a .231 average, nine strikeouts, and five errors. An Associated Press article excoriated Abstein for his poor play.

"During the games with Detroit Abstein appeared to forget all that he knew about baseball. He ran the bases foolishly, made a number of costly errors, failed to hit and disobeyed orders. In fact, his playing was worse than that of any other man on either team. The other Pirates, seeing that Abstein was the 'goat' for the combination, kept up the cry against him...Before the series was ended many of the Pirates shunned Abstein and it was reported he would be traded."[11]

Just over a month later it was reported that the Pirates coveted New York Giants first baseman Fred Tenney, a soon-to-be 38-year-old who paced the senior circuit in plate appearances and runs in 1908, but whose best days were behind him. "[Fred] Clarke sent word to a friend here recently that he still considered Tenney the peer of any man in the National League at first base," wrote the New York Times.[12]

Instead of landing Tenney, the Pirates purchased John Flynn from St. Paul, who would go on to lead Pittsburgh in homers in

1910 with six. Abstein was claimed off waivers by his hometown St. Louis Browns, but failed miserably in a brief trial that saw him hit .149 in 25 games and commit 11 errors in 23 games at first base. He spent the next seven years in the minors before calling it quits in 1916 at age 33.

Hello, Goodbye: Reb Russell's "Perfect" Game

Going into Game Five of the 1917 World Series against the New York Giants, White Sox manager Clarence "Pants" Rowland had a decision to make—give the ball to staff ace Eddie Cicotte for the third time in the Series, or send southpaw Reb Russell to the hill for his first start since September 24. The Series was tied at two games apiece, Chicago having won the first two contests at Comiskey Park, the Giants having won Games Three and Four at the Polo Grounds.

After scoring seven runs in Game Two, the White Sox were shut out by Rube Benton and Ferdie Schupp, and had gone 22 straight innings without scoring a run. According to newspapers, the Giants were "chipper and confident" going into the fifth game, and feared none of the White Sox hurlers.[1] "We have beaten Cicotte," proclaimed Giants second baseman and team captain Buck Herzog, "and we can beat him and that shine ball any time he goes against us."[2]

Cicotte had actually beaten the Giants in Game One, allowing one earned run in a complete game 2-1 victory over Slim Sallee, but lost Game Three despite surrendering only two runs in eight innings and striking out eight. Russell had gone 15-5 with a 1.95

ERA during the regular season and went 9-1 in his last 10 decisions with a save. But he appeared in only 35 games after averaging 47 from 1913 to 1916, thanks to a sore arm he developed in March.[3]

He wanted a crack at the Giants and "told everybody on the train that all through the National League season the New York club had its troubles whenever a good left-hander showed any speed and curves."[4] Apparently the weather factored into each manager's decision and it was speculated that Giants skipper John McGraw would go with Pol Perritt if it was cold, and Rowland would tab Russell if it was damp.[5]

According to the *New York Times*, conditions for Game Five were "so cold that spectators and players shivered in the wintry blasts,"[6] yet McGraw sent Sallee to the mound despite claims that he was not a "good cold day pitcher."[7] Sallee was a lefthander and it was believed the Giants' plan was to "southpaw the Sox out of the series." Rowland went with Russell, who insisted that he'd beat the Giants.

Russell took the hill in the top of the first in what the *New York Times* described as "miserable baseball weather...overcoats and furs were needed to keep the fans from shivering in the stands."[9] Giants left fielder George Burns took four straight balls for a leadoff walk, then Russell surrendered a hit-and-run single to Buck Herzog that put runners on first and third. Rowland wasn't taking any chances and had Eddie Cicotte and Lefty Williams begin warming up.

White Sox southpaw Reb Russell faced only three batters in his Game Five start against the New York Giants, a record of futility for starting pitchers.

They didn't get long to loosen up. Benny Kauff, who tied a World Series record with two homers in Game Four, continued his hot hitting and "smashed Russell's first offering to the right field bleachers, scoring Burns and putting Herzog on third."[10] Russell was promptly removed in favor of Cicotte, and thus ended the shortest outing in World Series History.

"In less than two minutes, Rowland discovered his mistake," wrote Irving Sanborn, "for the only thing Russell could get past the bats of the enemy was a bad ball."[11] Cicotte escaped the jam with only one more run coming home, and the Giants jumped out to a quick 2-0 lead. The White Sox cut the lead in half with a run in the third, but New York plated two more in the fourth to go up 4-1. Again Chicago halved New York's lead in the sixth, thanks to consecutive singles by Buck Weaver, Ray Schalk and Swede Risberg, who was pinch hitting for Cicotte.

After six strong innings in which he allowed just one earned run, Cicotte's day was done. Rowland called on Williams to tame the Giants in the seventh, but an Art Fletcher lead-off double followed by Bill Rariden's run-scoring single put the McGraws up by three again at 5-2. "There wasn't anything to yell about until the end of the seventh," wrote James Crusinberry about the Comiskey Park throng, "and although the Sox were on the field battling for the championship of the world and were being thoroughly licked for the first two-thirds of the game, the crowd kept still."

In fact, according to Sanborn the Sox faithful were so fed up by their team's sloppy play, they were actually rooting for the Giants through the first four innings.[13] But Chicago mounted a late comeback, scoring three in the bottom of the seventh to knot the game at 5-5, and the "almost 30,000 strong, cut loose and rejoiced in a loud voice."[14] "Shoeless Joe" Jackson and Happy Felsch laced consecutive one-out singles to put runners on first and third, before Chick Gandil doubled to knock in both of them. Weaver moved

Gandil to third with a groundout and the latter came home on a double steal that the Giants misplayed into a run.

"I did not think those steel and concrete stands were going to hold up under the tremendous pounding they received from the mad rooters," wrote Sanborn, "who danced and jumped and yelled and threw in the air everything that was close."[15] Red Faber took over mound duties for the White Sox and silenced New York's bats for the final two innings. The White Sox plated three more runs in the bottom of the eighth off Sallee and Perritt, and took Game Five by a count of 8-5. They also won Game Six in New York, 4-2, and captured their second championship in 12 years.

Reb Russell never pitched in another World Series game and is one of a handful of pitchers to own a career World Series ERA of infinity.

The Ultimate Fall Classic: Game Two

October 9, 1916—Brooklyn Robins at Boston Red Sox: Heading into the 1916 World Series, the Boston Red Sox were one of the two premier teams in the brief history of the American League. If they could defeat Brooklyn, they'd have their fourth championship and would supplant the Philadelphia Athletics as the AL's top team.

Meanwhile, the Brooklyn Robins had copped their first NL pennant of the modern era on the strength of a 94-60 record, and led their respective league in wins for the first time since 1900. The Robins had averaged only 67 wins a year since 1901 and finished in the second division 12 times in 14 seasons before finishing third in 1915 and copping their first flag a year later.

It wasn't surprising then that most figured Boston would win with relative ease. On paper the Robins were much more formidable than they were getting credit for. They averaged 3.75 runs per game on offense, good for third in the NL; allowed 2.99 runs per game, second best in the NL; sported the league's best ERA at 2.12; and boasted the league's most efficient defense.

The Red Sox, on the other hand, had only the sixth best offense in the AL, scoring 3.51 runs per game; allowed a league-best 3.08 runs per game; sported the second best ERA in the junior circuit at 2.48; and boasted the league's best defense, in both efficiency and fielding percentage.

After dealing Tris Speaker to the Indians in the offseason, Boston had few real stars on offense. Third baseman Larry Gardner batted .308 with a team-leading 62 RBIs; right fielder Harry Hooper paced the team with 75 runs, 27 steals, and 11 triples; center fielder Tilly Walker smacked 29 doubles, 11 triples, and three homers, tying for first place in all three categories. But the team hit only 14 round-trippers all year.

The Robins boasted more power and speed than Boston, hitting twice as many homers as the Sox and stealing 58 more bases. Most of Brooklyn's production came from their corner outfielders, left fielder Zack Wheat, who batted .312 with nine homers and 73 RBIs, and paced the team in just about every offensive category, and right fielder Casey Stengel, who belted eight homers and drove in 53 runs. First baseman Jake Daubert batted a team-high .316 and stole 21 bases; and second baseman George Cutshaw led the team with 27 steals.

Most experts gave the Red Sox an edge in pitching. Twenty-one-year-old southpaw Babe Ruth was the ace of the Red Sox staff after going 23-12 with a 1.75 ERA and nine shutouts, leading the American League in the latter two categories. Another southpaw, 24-year-old Dutch Leonard, went 18-12 with a 2.36 ERA and was only two years removed from his record-setting 0.96 earned run average in 1914. Submariner Carl Mays also won 18 games and posted a 2.39 ERA while bouncing around between the rotation and bullpen. Ernie Shore went 16-10 with a 2.63 ERA, and Rube Foster was 14-7 with a 3.06 mark.

The Robins had a strong staff of their own that boasted better depth than Boston's mound corps. Right-hander Jeff Pfeffer went 25-11 with a 1.92 ERA; Larry Cheney, a spitball artist, went 18-12 with a 1.92 ERA and finished second in the NL in strikeouts with 166. Southpaw Sherry Smith won 14 games and boasted a 2.34 ERA; lefty Rube Marquard won only 13 games, but posted a 1.58 ERA, second in the league only to Grover Cleveland Alexander; 33-year-old veteran Jack Coombs went 13-8 with a 2.66 ERA; and Wheezer Dell posted a 2.26 ERA in 32 appearances, half of which came as a starter.

Still, most experts were higher on Boston's staff. "I think [Red Sox manager] Bill Carrigan has one of the finest pitching staffs ever carried in the big leagues," wrote Giants manager John McGraw, "and there is no more competent handler of the talent...Carrigan will win the series on his pitchers if he wins at all."[1] Oddsmakers had Boston favored to win the Series, with odds shifting daily.

Despite a valiant comeback that saw Brooklyn score four runs in the ninth inning of Game One, the Red Sox held on for a 6-5 win to take a 1-0 lead in the Series. The Robins outhit the Red Sox, 10-8, but only two of them went for extra-bases, triples by Chief Meyers and Wheat, while Boston pounded out five extra-base hits, three doubles and two triples, all off Marquard. Brooklyn also committed four errors to Boston's one.

After playing the first game on Saturday, there was no game on Sunday, and the Series commenced on Monday at Braves Field. Red Sox owner Joe Lannin had rented the stadium for the World Series because it had a larger capacity than Fenway Park. Typically the National Commission would flip a coin to decide where the first game of the World Series would be played, but Lannin appealed to the Commission and suggested that starting the Series in Boston on Saturday and playing Game Two on Monday would give the Robins more time to sell tickets to their fans for the first game at Ebbets Field on October 10.[2]

The Commission agreed to begin the Series in Boston and the move to Braves Field paid off when 36,117 fans came to see Game One, and 47,373 patrons packed the grounds for Game Two.

Ruth was scheduled to pitch for Boston, but newspapers listed Cheney, Smith, or Coombs as Brooklyn's expected hurler. Hugh

Fullerton thought it would be a mistake to throw Cheney against batters who were used to facing spitballs on a regular basis. "[Robinson] plans to shoot Cheney at the Red Sox tomorrow, which is much the same as shooting him at sunrise," the writer joked.[3]

After all the speculation and guessing, Robinson tabbed Smith to take the hill for Brooklyn. Smith featured a curve, fastball, changeup, and knuckler, and was said to have the best pickoff move of his time. "They used to say about Sherry Smith that if the base runner was only thinking about taking a lead Sherry would throw over and get him between thoughts," wrote former umpire Jocko Conlan in 1967.[4]

The Robins wasted little time putting a run on the board when with two outs and nobody on in the first, center fielder Hi Myers belted one between Tilly Walker and Harry Hooper that rolled all the way to the center field fence, allowing Myers to circle the bases with an inside-the-park home run. "Myers alone found the one system to foil this foe," wrote Grantland Rice, "a drive that no man could stop who was not accompanied by a taxicab or a 60-foot net."[5]

Smith retired the side in order with no trouble in the bottom of the first, then Ruth returned the favor in the top of the second. Duffy Lewis earned Boston's first hit of the game with a one-out single to center in the bottom of the second, but was forced at second on a Gardner groundout. Catcher Otto Miller picked Gardner off first to end the frame.

Boston's defense saved Ruth in the top of the third when shortstop Everett Scott made a nice play on a Miller grounder for the first out, and Hooper, Walker and Scott followed with a brilliant play, in which Hooper retrieved Smith's long drive to right and threw to Walker, who relayed the ball to Scott covering third. Smith had an easy double but attempted to stretch the hit into a triple and was tagged out. Johnston followed with a single to center that would have surely plated Smith with Brooklyn's second run, then was gunned down at second by catcher Pinch Thomas on a steal attempt to end the inning.

The Red Sox tied the score in the bottom of the third when Scott tripled, then came home on Ruth's one-out grounder to Cutshaw. After that, both hurlers settled down and went to work. Ruth walked Daubert to lead off the fourth, which forced Carrigan to begin warming up Foster, but Scott, Janvrin, and Hoblitzel turned a nifty 6-4-3 double play, and Ruth coaxed Wheat to ground back to the box to end the inning. Not to be outdone, the Robins turned a double play of their own in the bottom of the fourth.

Ruth surrendered a two-out single to shortstop Ivy Olson in the top of the fifth, but Miller flied out to Hooper to end the inning. Then the bottom of the fifth got a little hairy. With two outs, Thomas slammed a shot to left and took off around the bases. As he rounded second, he was tripped by Olson, who was charged with interference, and Thomas was awarded third base.

Olson began to argue with the umpires, then turned his attention to Red Sox player-coach Heinie Wagner, who had a few choice words for Olson. The men were separated by home plate umpire and former Red Sox World Series hero Bill Dinneen and order was restored. Thomas was stranded on third when Ruth whiffed on three straight pitches.

In the top of the sixth, Ruth walked Johnston with one out, but he was thrown out at second base by Thomas for the second time in the game on an apparent botched hit-and-run with Daubert at the plate. Daubert grounded to third to end the inning, then Myers made his presence felt a second time when he snared Hooper's low liner with a shoestring catch, and somersaulted to his feet with the ball in his glove. Those who saw it swore that had Myers missed, the ball would have rolled forever and Hooper would have had an easy home run. Janvrin and Walker were retired easily and the game went into the seventh still tied at 1-1 and neither team giving an inch.

Ruth retired the Robins in order in the top of the seventh, but not without a second round of arguing, as Myers was called out on a close play at first, prompting half of Brooklyn's dugout to spill onto the field in protest to no avail. Smith walked Hoblitzel to start the bottom of the seventh, but retired the next three men in order and the game remained knotted.

Brooklyn threatened to break the tie in the top of the eighth when Mowrey singled to left to lead off the frame, then advanced to second on an Olson sacrifice bunt. Miller singled to center to move Mowrey to third, where he stayed despite a poor throw from Tilly Walker that allowed Miller to move up to second and put runners on second and third. Then Ruth turned to his "horseshoes and four-leaf clovers,"[6] and coaxed Smith to ground to Scott, who fired to Thomas at home. Mowrey was caught in a rundown and finally retired by Ruth, who put the tag on him. Johnston grounded back to the mound and was thrown out at first to end Brooklyn's strongest threat since the first.

Smith remained cool and calm and retired the Sox in order again in the bottom of the eighth. Ruth did the same to the Robins, setting up a chance for the Red Sox to win the game in the bottom of the ninth. Janvrin gave the hometown throng hope when he doubled to lead off the inning, then Carrigan made a surprising move when he sent light-hitting, lefty swinging Jimmy Walsh to the plate instead of the right-handed Walker.

Walsh laid down a bunt and the Robins had a chance to retire Janvrin at third, but Mowrey couldn't handle the throw and everyone was safe. With runners on first and third and no outs, Myers came to the fore once again and made a spectacular play, snaring Hoblitzel's fly ball, then throwing a perfect strike to the plate to nab Janvrin by two feet. Walsh took second on the throw, but Lewis was intentionally walked and Gardner popped up to Miller to end the inning and send the game into extra frames.

Ruth sandwiched three groundouts around a two-out walk to Olson and handed the game back over to his teammates, who almost scored the winning run again in the bottom of the 10th, but fell short for the second straight stanza. With Everett Scott at second on a single and sacrifice and two outs, Hooper topped a slow dribbler to third, hit, according to Ring Lardner, "as hard as last summer's ice cream."[7]

Mowrey came in and fielded it cleanly, but knew he had no chance to throw out the runner at first, so he bluffed a throw, then spun and fired the ball to Olson, who had followed Scott to third. Scott rounded the bag too far and upon seeing Mowrey throw the ball in his direction, tried to scramble back to the bag, but slipped and fell, allowing Olson to apply the tag for the third out. It was, according to Fullerton, "the smartest and best inside play of the series."[8]

Ruth came out strong and retired the side in order in the 11th, fanning Daubert to end the inning, then Smith sandwiched two

Babe Ruth (far left) enjoyed one of the greatest pitching performances in Game Two of the 1916 Fall Classic.

popups and a groundout around a two-out walk to Hoblitzel, the third free pass Smith issued to "Hobby" in the contest.

Ruth continued to dominate the Robins, retiring the side in order in the 12th with a strikeout of Myers, a pop fly by Wheat, and a groundout to short by Cutshaw. Through 12 innings, Ruth had allowed only six hits and three walks, while fanning three, and hadn't allowed a hit since the eighth. Smith issued a one-out walk to Scott in the bottom of the inning, the hurler's fifth free pass of the game, but neither Thomas nor Ruth could bring him home, the latter grounding out weakly to the pitcher. In five trips to the plate, the Bambino managed to get only one ball past the infield, but had also knocked in the team's only run.

Brooklyn managed to get a runner to second base in the 13th, but Otto Miller popped out to Pinch Thomas, and Duffy Lewis made a sensational catch on a drive by Smith to end the inning. "Here Lewis saved the day," wrote Edward Martin. "He came in pell mell, rushing over toward left center and plucking from his shoe-tops a smash by Sherrod Smith, which was on its way to the fence in center. This was just about one of the niftiest little things seen at the home of big things."[9]

Smith continued to match Ruth pitch for pitch and set the Sox down in order in the bottom of the 13th, but the Boston southpaw was getting stronger with each extra frame and retired the Robins in order again. By the time the Red Sox went to bat in the bottom of the 14th darkness began to set in.

Hoblitzel drew his fourth walk of the game to lead off the inning. Lewis laid down a sacrifice bunt that moved Hoblitzel to second, then Carrigan made two moves that resulted in the game-winning tally, sending in Del Gainer to hit for Gardner, then, with one strike on the batter, putting in Mike McNally to pinch run for Hoblitzel.

"When they put Mike on second they practically announced publicly they are going to win the ball game," wrote Martin. "Out of the second hassock the Minooka speed king was all set to bring in the big run."[10]

With a 1-1 count on him, Gainer slashed Smith's third offering just past the outstretched glove of Mowrey and into left field. "'Ducky' slammed one and Minooka Mike was off like a flash," Martin continued. "The hit went out to Zacharia, but McNally had rounded third and was tearing for the counting station before Zack let his throw go. Minooka Mike beat it, scoring the run that won the old ball game..."[11]

Grantland Rice was especially poetic in his description of the game, giving most of the credit to Boston's glove men. "For 14 innings the Brooklyn attack, led by Hi Myers, stormed and hammered Boston's impregnable defense in a vain effort to cut a way through to the Promised Land. But for 14 innings this Boston defense formed a long, wide wall of steel and stone back of Babe Ruth...It was a wall of human flesh that shifted and swerved to meet every point of Brooklyn's blind, but game, aggressive attack."[12]

After the game, Ruth embraced Carrigan in a hug and roared, "I told you I could take care of those National League sons of bitches!"[13]

The Red Sox would go on to win the 1916 World Series in five games.

1920: A True Fall Classic

The months leading up to the 1920 World Series were riddled with controversy and among the most tumultuous in baseball history. In mid-August both leagues featured tight pennant races, especially in the junior circuit where the Cleveland Indians held a miniscule .004 point lead over the Chicago White Sox while the New York Yankees stood only a half-game off the pace. Over in the National League the Brooklyn Robins boasted a one-game lead over the defending champion Cincinnati Reds and a three-game cushion over the New York Giants.

On Monday, August 16 the Yankees hosted the Indians at the Polo Grounds for the first of a crucial three-game series. With Cleveland leading the Yanks, 3-0, heading into the fifth inning against submarine hurler Carl Mays, things took a turn for the tragic when Mays beaned popular shortstop Ray Chapman. Chapman had to be helped to the clubhouse and was eventually taken to the hospital where it was revealed he had a fractured skull. Surgery was performed to relieve pressure on his brain, but he died early the next morning.

Then on September 7 the Cook County, Illinois grand jury announced it would investigate gambling in baseball after being made aware of a plot by Chicago Cubs pitcher Claude Hendrix to throw a game against the Philadelphia Phillies on August 31. Hendrix had allegedly bet against his own team, but he was yanked from the rotation after Cubs owner Bill Veeck Sr. received tips that the game had been fixed. Grover Cleveland Alexander got the start instead. The Cubs still lost, 3-0, and Hendrix was released and effectively blackballed by the rest of Major League Baseball.

On September 23, it was reported that not only had the Cubs-Phillies game been tainted, the 1919 World Series had also been fixed.[1] During testimony, American League President Ban Johnson dropped a bombshell when he testified that the White Sox were also throwing the 1920 pennant to the Cleveland Indians.

"I heard several weeks ago a vague statement that the White Sox would not dare win the pennant this season...because the gambling syndicate would tell what they knew of the conduct of certain players in the...World's championship games in 1919," Johnson claimed.[2] When the report came out Chicago was only a half-game back of Cleveland with only 10 days left in the regular season. Clean members of the White Sox backed up Johnson's claim and swore that some of their teammates "regulated their playing...by the score board, winning or losing as the occasion demanded in order to keep the betting odds favorable...If Cleveland won, we won. If Cleveland lost, we lost."[3]

Eight White Sox players were implicated in the gambling scandal and seven were suspended by team owner Charles Comiskey with three games to go. Among them was the heart of the team—starting outfielders Joe Jackson and Happy Felsch, third baseman Buck Weaver, shortstop Swede Risberg, pitchers Eddie Cicotte and Lefty Williams, and infielder Fred McMullin.[4]

Still only a half-game back of first with three to go, the White Sox lost two of three to the St. Louis Browns while the Indians split a four-game set with Detroit to finish two games ahead of Chicago and three ahead of the Yankees, and captured their first pennant in franchise history. The Brooklyn Robins, on the other hand, began putting the NL flag on ice on September 9 with a 4-2 win over the St. Louis Cardinals, and finished with a comfortable seven-game edge over the second-place Giants.

The World Series was to be a best-of-nine affair scheduled to begin in Cleveland, but the first three games were played at Brooklyn's Ebbets Field while League Park was being renovated to add more seats for the Fall Classic. Before the games could begin, however, a ruling needed to be made about Cleveland's roster. Under the rules, a player added to a team's roster after September 1 was ineligible to play in the World Series, which put the Indians over a barrel. When Chapman died they had little choice but to use light-hitting Harry Lunte at shortstop until New Orleans Pelican star and future Hall of Famer Joe Sewell was ready to be promoted.

In 19 games between Chapman's death and Sewell's debut, Lunte batted .200 with no extra base hits, but played very good defense and fielded at a .979 clip. After making his debut on September 10, Sewell showed he was a superior hitter, batting .329 in 22 games, but he was terrible in the field, committing 15 errors for an .884 fielding percentage. Still, the Indians were hoping the National Commission would grant them permission to use Sewell in the World Series.

The Commission allowed Brooklyn owner Charles Ebbets to decide whether Sewell should be eligible. "Whether because of public pressure or a strong sense of sportsmanship," wrote author Mike Sowell, "the Brooklyn owner approved Sewell's addition to the Cleveland roster."[5]

Much of the talk surrounding the Series had to do with two other roster spots, one held by Indians first baseman Wheeler "Doc" Johnston and the other by younger brother Jimmy Johnston, who manned third base for the Robins. Legendary writer Ring Lardner had some fun at the brothers' expense when he wrote about a new World Series scandal that pitted brothers against each other for the first time in Fall Classic history.

"The fact that Doc ain't called by his real name which is Wheeler and the fact that Jim was born in Cleveland [Tennessee] and is now playing with Brooklyn is both of them suspicious," joked Lardner. "Doc was born in 1889. Both men is [sic] very fast, but if Jim had of been a year faster they would of [sic] been twins."[6] They might not have been twins, but the Johnston brothers were almost identical hitters in 1920—Doc batted .292/.333/.385; Jimmy batted .291/.338/.361.

Twenty-four-game winner and spitball artist Stan Coveleski got the ball for the Indians in Game One and was brilliant, scattering five hits in a 3-1 win over Rube Marquard. Another spitballer twirled a gem in Game Two when Brooklyn ace Burleigh Grimes shut out the Indians, 3-0, to even the Series. Southpaw Sherry Smith held Cleveland to one unearned run on three hits in a Game Three 2-1 win, but the Indians tied the Series at two games apiece on another masterpiece by Coveleski, who replicated his Game One performance with another one-run-on-five-hits outing.

Then things got historic in Game Five. Jim Bagby, who led the AL in wins with 31, win/loss percentage, games, innings, and complete games, matched up with Game Two winner Burleigh Grimes again and this time things were very different. Despite allowing 13 hits, only one—an Ed Konetchy triple in the second inning—went for extra bases, and Bagby surrendered one run in nine innings.

He was staked to an early 4-0 lead in the first when Charlie Jamieson, Bill Wambsganns, and Tris Speaker rapped out consecutive singles to load the bases for the team's leading home run hitter, Elmer Smith, who finished fifth in the AL with 12 circuit clouts. According to James O'Leary of the *Boston Globe*, Smith looked like the "veriest busher" when he missed Grimes' first two offerings by a foot, but he measured a one ball, two strike pitch "which he pickled and sent high over the right field fence" for a grand slam, the first ever hit in a World Series.[7]

Bagby held Brooklyn scoreless through the first four innings, then helped himself when he belted a three-run homer into League Park's temporary center field stands to give him and his teammates a 7-0 lead in the bottom of the fourth. It was the first time a pitcher had homered in a World Series. But the firsts didn't end there. In fact, neither did the lasts.

Perhaps still giddy from and distracted by his home run, Bagby put the first two men on in the top of the fifth when he allowed singles to second baseman Pete Kilduff and catcher Otto Miller to lead off the fifth inning. That brought up pitcher Clarence Mitchell, who had replaced Grimes in the bottom of the fourth, and who could wield a bat better than he could sling a baseball. Mitchell hit .367 in 1919 and would go on to hit .290 and drive in 28 runs in 56 games in 1922, and Brooklyn skipper Wilbert Robinson was counting on him to supply a spark.

Robinson called for a hit-and-run and Mitchell "connected solidly and jammed a tearing liner over second base," according to the *New York Times*. "[Bill Wambsganns] was quite a distance from second, but he leaped over toward the cushion and with a mighty jump speared the ball with one hand."[8] Kilduff and Miller were off with the pitch and each had almost reached third and second, respectively, when Wambsganns corralled the drive.

"Wamby's noodle began to operate faster than it ever did before," continued the *Times*. "He hopped over to second and touched the bag, retiring Kilduff, who was far down the alley toward third base. Then Wamby turned and saw Otto Miller standing there like a wooden Indian. Otto was evidently so surprised that he was glued to the ground, and Wamby just waltzed over and touched him for the third out."[9]

Depending on who you believe, this was either the second or third unassisted triple play in major league history, but definitely the first and only one in World Series play.[10] Cleveland waltzed to an easy 8-1 win, then took the last two games by scores of 1-0 behind Duster Mails, and 3-0 on yet another five-hitter by Stan Coveleski, who finished the Series with a 3-0 record and an outstanding 0.67 ERA.

It would be 16 years before another hitter would hit a grand slam in World Series play (Tony Lazzeri in 1936), but only four before another pitcher homered in a World Series and the trick was turned twice in three days by teammates Rosy Ryan and Jack Bentley, who homered for the Giants in Games Three and Five, respectively, in 1924. Another Giant played a role in a milestone when outfielder Irish Meusel squared off against his brother Bob of the Yankees in 1921, 1922, and 1923. Irish led the '21 and '22 Fall Classics in RBIs with seven in each, and Bob paced everyone in ribbies with eight in 1923.

Scalped by More Than the Indians

Although his best years were behind him, 33-year-old 13-year veteran lefty Rube Marquard helped the Brooklyn Robins win the

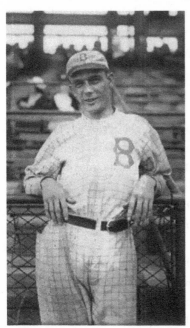

Hall of Fame hurler Rube Marquard was run out of Brooklyn after a run-in with the law during the 1920 World Series.

National League pennant in 1920 when he went 10-7 with a 3.23 ERA in 28 games. He started the first game of the World Series against the Cleveland Indians and lost 3-1, allowing all three runs in only six innings of work. Then he tossed three scoreless innings in relief in Game Four, a 5-1 Brooklyn loss. They would prove to be the last frames Marquard would throw in the postseason.

Prior to Game Four the southpaw was arrested in the lobby of the Hotel Winton in Cleveland when he was caught trying to scalp tickets, a set of box seats with a face value of $52.80 for which

Marquard paid $275 and was asking $350.[1] Marquard was released on his own recognizance and ordered to appear in court the following Monday.

"The police say that they would have held him in custody if it had not been for the fact that they did not want to be accused of trying to cripple the Brooklyn club while it is playing in the world's series here," reported the *New York Times*.[2]

When Robins manager Wilbert Robinson learned of Marquard's arrest "he is alleged to have said that he would not give 5 cents to get him out of hock."[3] But when Leon Cadore and Al Mamaux allowed four runs in the first two innings, Marquard was summoned into the game in the third inning and pitched through the fifth. After Game Six on October 11, a 1-0 Cleveland win, National League president John Heydler announced that Marquard's World Series share would be withheld until his case was settled. When asked what kind of penalty Marquard would incur from the league if he was found guilty, Heydler insisted it would be "plenty stiff enough to make Mr. Marquard wish he'd never seen a World's Series ticket."[4]

The Indians wrapped up the best-of-eight Series with a 3-0 win in Game Seven on October 12, and Marquard was found guilty of ticket scalping and incurred a $1 fine and costs, making his total fine $3.80.[5] The judge was lenient because he felt the negative press Marquard received was punishment enough.[6] But Marquard was persona non grata as far as Brooklyn owner Charles Ebbets was concerned.

"I'm through with him absolutely," Ebbets spat. "He hasn't been released, however, and if anyone else wants him he can have him. But Marquard will never again put on a Brooklyn uniform."[7] Neither Heydler nor the National Commission took further action, although it was speculated that Marquard would be "railroaded" out of the National League.[8]

To add insult to injury, Marquard's wife, Vaudeville star Blossom Seeley, asked for a divorce on October 15 on the grounds that Marquard had deserted her in 1918.[9] Once the smoke cleared and the dust settled, Marquard was traded to the Cincinnati Reds on December 15, 1920 for pitcher Dutch Ruether. He spent only a year with the Reds, then pitched for the Boston Braves from 1922-1925 before calling it a career.

He went 201-177 with a 3.08 ERA in 18 seasons and was inducted into the Hall of Fame by the Veteran's Committee in 1971.

Jesse Haines Out-Babes "The Babe"

Most baseball fans know that before he became arguably the greatest hitter in baseball history, George Herman "Babe" Ruth was one of the best pitchers and on his way to becoming one of the all-time great mound artists. So it's no surprise that Ruth went 3-0 with a 0.87 ERA in World Series play, nor is it shocking that he hit .326 and slugged .744 in 41 Fall Classic games. But he was supposed to do that, right?

Hall of Famer Jesse "Pop" Haines also had a very good career, winning 210 games over 19 years and finishing eighth in MVP voting in 1927 after going 24-10 for the St. Louis Cardinals and leading the National League in complete games with 25 and shutouts with six. But Haines was one of the worst hitting pitchers of his era, finishing with a career batting average of .186 and only three home runs in 1,124 at-bats. Through the 1926 season the then-33-year-old had batted a measly .187 with one lone homer in almost 600 at-bats.

With Ruth's Yankees facing Haines' Cardinals in the 1926 World Series, it was almost fitting that these two should clash; the greatest slugger of all-time vs. a man who couldn't hit if his life depended on it. In Game One, Ruth went 1 for 3 with a run and a walk. Haines pitched the bottom of the eighth and retired Ruth, Lou Gehrig, and

Tony Lazzeri around a walk to Bob Meusel. The Yanks took the first tilt, 2-1, at Yankee Stadium.

Grover Cleveland Alexander evened the Series at one game apiece when he fanned 10 in a 6-2 win in Game Two. Then it was Haines' turn and he made the most of it. He retired the first six batters he faced before surrendering a single to Joe Dugan in the third inning. He worked his way out of a two-on, two-out jam in that frame, then stranded Ruth at second in the fourth.

Yankees southpaw Dutch Ruether wasn't as efficient—he put runners on base in each of the first three innings—but he had yet to allow a run either. In the bottom of the fourth, St. Louis plated the first run on a Les Bell single, a sacrifice, and a throwing error by shortstop Mark Koenig. Then Haines flexed his muscles and popped a two-run homer into the right field seats to stake his club to a 3-0 lead.

According to Grantland Rice, the fans broke out in a "vocal riot" following Haines' four-bagger. "It was a cataclysm of sound that went roaring on its way to the Ozarks," he wrote, "and is still reverberating through the wildwoods of these historic knobs."[1] Haines was far less poetic when discussing his first homer in six years. "It was a long time to wait, but gee, it was great when it came."[2]

The hurler's unexpected blast effectively ended the day for the Yankees. Haines stifled them on only five hits "as badly scattered as Jack Dempsey's man-killing blows..." and shut out the Bronx Bombers in a 4-0 win.[3] He became the first pitcher to homer in a World Series game in which he also pitched a complete game shutout, and only Bucky Walters (1940) was able to match the feat.

Not surprisingly, Ruth dominated at the plate, belting four homers and walking 11 times in seven games, but the Cardinals won their first World Series since being admitted into the National League in 1892, with Haines earning the win in Game Seven with help from Alexander. He smacked another hit in the final tilt and finished 3 for 5 with a homer, two RBIs and a run scored.

He faced the Yankees again in 1928, but lost Game Three and went 0 for 2. In 1930 Haines outdueled A's legend Lefty Grove in a 3-1 Game Four victory, and went 1 for 2 with an RBI. His last hurrah came in 1934 when the 41-year-old fanned two of the three batters he faced in the eighth inning of Game Four against the Detroit Tigers.

When all was said and done, Jesse Haines finished his postseason career with a record of 3-1 and a 1.67 ERA, and batted .444 with a .778 slugging percentage.

The Ultimate Fall Classic: Game Three

October 3, 1919—Cincinnati Reds at Chicago White Sox: By the end of the 1919 season, the White Sox were regarded as one of the best teams in American League history. Twenty-five years after the 1919 season ended, sportswriters still considered them one of the top two teams of all time, placing them second to the '27 Yankees.

The Reds, on the other hand, were in their first World Series. American League teams had won eight of the previous nine World Series, including a 4-2 victory by the White Sox over the New York Giants just two years prior. Needless to say, the Reds were not expected to be able to break the AL's monopoly on the title.

Rumors that the White Sox were going to throw the World Series to the Reds began to surface even before Sox ace Eddie Cicotte plunked Reds second baseman Morrie Rath with his second offering to lead off the bottom of the first inning of the first game. The strategically placed pitch allegedly served as a signal to gamblers that key members of the White Sox team had agreed to throw the Series.

The Reds pounded Cicotte in Game One for six runs on seven hits and two walks in only 3 2/3 innings. They scored three more runs off Roy Wilkinson and Grover Lowdermilk to easily take the first contest, 9-1, behind the fantastic hurling of Dutch Ruether, who allowed only one unearned run on six hits in nine innings. At the time, the eight-run margin of victory was the largest ever in the first game of a World Series.

Things got worse for Chicago when Game Two starter, Lefty Williams, melted down in the fourth inning when he issued three walks and surrendered two hits in a three-run inning that effectively put the game on ice. Williams, who finished fourth in the AL in fewest walks per nine innings during the regular season at 1.76, handed out six free passes in eight innings of work en route to a 4-2 loss that put the Pale Hose in a two-game hole going into Game Three. Four of the six men Williams walked came around to score.

Prior to the start of the Series, Cicotte demanded $10,000 for his part in the conspiracy. He found the money under his hotel room pillow. He didn't know where it came from or who put it there. It didn't matter. The fix was on.

Of all the games they were most likely to throw, the third tilt was the one. The players insisted there was no way they'd win for rookie pitcher Dickey Kerr, whom they called a "Busher." Kerr, who was starting in the absence of an injured and ill Red Faber, faced nine-year veteran right-hander Ray Fisher, a spitballer who went 14-5 with a 2.17 ERA in his first year with the Reds after spending eight years with the Yankees.

Harvey Woodruff of the *Chicago Tribune* wrote, "We are two down with seven to go. The situation has driven all the advance confidence or over-confidence out of both [White Sox] players and their followers. Only an optimistic detective could find a White Sox smile anywhere in this city tonight...Defeat for the Sox tomorrow will reduce chances of ultimate success, almost to a minimum, while victory will mean much at this time. It is the crisis of the series up to this point."[1]

The diminutive Kerr was no pushover. The 25-year-old rookie southpaw went 13-7 with a 2.88 ERA, bouncing back and forth between the rotation and the bullpen. He completed 10 of his 17 starts and finished second in the AL in games finished with 20. Kerr's performance was somewhat of a surprise to Damon Runyon, who once described the pitcher as, "Too small for too much of anything, except, perhaps, a watch charm..."[2]

According to Harvey Woodruff, when the White Sox took the field for the top of the first inning, they received a warm welcome from their fans. "When the Sox appeared on the field there was a roar of applause that showed Sox rooters are no more quitters than their team...It undoubtedly nerved and braced the already determined Gleasons," wrote Woodruff.[3]

Kerr was masterful in the first, effectively mixing his pitches and retiring the side in order on a groundout by Morrie Rath, a flyout by Jake Daubert, and a strikeout of Heinie Groh on four pitches. Fisher was almost as good and even more efficient, using only nine pitches to get out of the bottom of the first. Right fielder Nemo Leibold led off with a line shot to right that Greasy Neale snared off his shoe tops for the first out. "The slippery one scooted in for the ball as it was within about an inch of the ground," W. O. McGeehan wrote later. "One paw intercepted it and Neale rolled over and over, but he held the ball."[4] Eddie Collins bounced an easy grounder back to the mound for out number two, and Buck Weaver lofted a pop up to Daubert to retire the side.

Kerr allowed his first hit of the day with one out in the second on a Pat Duncan Texas League blooper to right center, but retired Edd Roush, Larry Kopf, and Neale on groundouts. Kerr used only nine pitches and seemed to have Reds batters baffled from the start. "He seemed to understand that his job was to put more stuff on the ball than the Reds had on their bats," wrote Grantland Rice, "and with this estimable purpose in view he cut away all wasted motion and began to stand the Reds upon their closely cropped heads."[5]

Fisher wasn't up to the task in the second and the White Sox broke through for two runs on two hits and an error. "The climax, which happened all too prematurely, came as the wind from the stock yards laden with life-giving balsam to the White Sox wafted over the diamond," wrote McGeehan. "It tickled the nostrils of Joe Jackson, the first of the Sox to bat in the second inning."[6] Shoeless Joe led off the inning with a single to left, then advanced to third when Fisher fielded Felsch's sacrifice bunt and threw it into center field trying to get Jackson at second. Felsch also advanced an extra base and the White Sox had runners at second and third with no outs.

"It so happened that just before cracking one at Felsch," Rice wrote, "Fisher had anointed the ball with a saliva dressing and as a certain soothsayer of renown once remarked, 'The evil that men do lives after them.' He must have nabbed the ball upon the slippery sector, for with an easy double play in sight, he pegged the ball far and high above Rath's quivering reach..."[7]

Ironically, Chick Gandil, the man who insisted the players involved in the gambling conspiracy would never win for a "busher," plated the first two runs of the game with a single to right, then advanced to second on Neale's throw to the plate, which might have nabbed Felsch had catcher Bill Rariden played it properly. Swede Risberg walked to put runners at first and second. But the pitcher forced Gandil at third on Ray Schalk's bunt and saved himself from further embarrassment.

Hugh Fullerton claimed that Gandil loafed on the play in an effort to kill the White Sox's rally, and the movie *Eight Men Out* depicted Gandil taking his sweet time getting to third base. "Gandil, coming up from second, had the play beaten by a block," wrote Fullerton, "but he stood up and seemed to be conversing with Kid Gleason (coaching at third base), when Fisher suddenly grabbed the ball and flashed it to Groh."[8] Christy Mathewson credited Fisher with making a great play, but admitted that Gandil might have helped the Reds by not sliding into the bag.[9] No other writer that I could find blamed Gandil for poor or suspicious base running, all crediting Fisher with a heads up play.

With Risberg at second and Schalk on first, Fisher coaxed a grounder by Kerr back to the box, and the Reds hurler threw again to Groh for the force out. Then Groh speared Leibold's grounder and threw him out at first to end the inning.

Kerr took the hill for the third inning and kept the ball down in the zone, getting Bill Rariden to ground to Weaver for the first out. Fisher tried to atone for his error by singling, but it was hardly an impressive belt. He topped a grounder toward third that Weaver backed away from in hopes that it would roll foul, but in his enthusiasm, Kerr raced over to field the ball and fell on top of it in fair territory. Kerr quickly recovered, though, and got Rath and Daubert to retire the side.

In the bottom of the third Collins smoked a single just past the outstretched glove of Kopf, and Weaver followed with a hit-and-run bloop single to a spot vacated by Kopf when the Reds shortstop went to second to cover the bag on Collins' steal attempt. Cincinnati was able to keep Collins at second and Weaver at first, however, which proved to be the White Sox's undoing. After Weaver's hit, Reds skipper Pat Moran ordered Hod Eller and "closer" Dolf Luque to start warming up.

Jackson, who was by far the team's best hitter that year and one of the best in the history of the league, stepped to the plate with a chance to stake Kerr to a bigger lead, but Gleason employed a Deadball Era play and ordered his slugger to lay down a sacrifice bunt to advance the runners. The play wasn't foreign to Jackson or any of the White Sox for that matter; they had sacrificed a league-leading 224 times and the "Shoeless One" had done so 17 times that year. Jackson wasn't able to get the ball down, however, instead popping it up over Fisher's head for what looked like a hit. But Daubert raced in from first and snagged the weak fly before it hit the ground. One batter later, Fisher's defense saved him again when Groh stopped Felsch's smash to third, picked it up and threw to Rath, who relayed to Daubert for a nifty inning-ending double play.

Thus began the fourth. Kerr walked Groh to lead off the frame, then Roush slapped a grounder past Kerr's glove, but Risberg raced in, grabbed it, and nipped Roush at first with a strong throw. Groh advanced to second on the play, but was retired when Duncan lined out to Risberg, who flipped the ball to Collins to complete the double play.

The White Sox shortstop played a key role in the bottom of the inning as well when he tripled to right with one out. "Risberg hit a long one to right field and Greasy Neale became depressed and befogged by the local ozone," quipped McGeehan. "The ball rolled by the greasy one for a three-bagger."[10] O'Leary insisted it would have gone for only two bases had Neale played it properly,[11] but none of the Sox or their fans complained when Risberg came home on Schalk's successful squeeze bunt, which eluded Fisher and went for a single. Rariden gunned down Schalk on a steal attempt for the second out of the inning, and Kerr grounded out to Kopf at short to end the threat.

With a three-run lead in the top of the fifth, Kerr surrendered his first solid hit of the game, a hard grounder by Kopf that sped into right field. That would be the highlight of the Reds' afternoon. Neale grounded to Gandil, who fired the ball to Risberg for the force at second; Rariden grounded to Collins, who threw to first for the out, Neale advancing to second on the play; Fisher grounded to Weaver at third, who tossed across to Gandil to end the inning.

Fisher had no trouble in the bottom of the fifth, retiring Leibold, Collins, and Weaver on three ground balls, the last two easy tappers back to the mound that Fisher handled himself. In the top of the sixth, Gandil made a nifty catch of Risberg's wide throw to retire Rath; Daubert lofted a routine fly to Jackson, and Weaver fielded Groh's grounder and tossed him out at first. Still 3-0 in favor of Chicago, the contest got heated in the bottom of the sixth and had cooler heads not prevailed, things could have gotten ugly.

It appeared that the bad blood began during Jackson's at-bat to lead off the bottom of the sixth, but the truth is things had been chippy between the clubs from the start. Jimmy Smith, a 24-year-old little-used utility infielder had been riding Eddie Collins from the Reds' bench since Game One, and Collins had had just about enough of Smith's chatter. He held his tongue and kept his composure, though.

But Jackson and Fisher took it to the next level in the sixth.

"Busher" Dickey Kerr wasn't supposed to beat the Cincinnati Reds in Game Three of the 1919 World Series, but he surprised everyone, including gamblers who bet on the White Sox to lose.

When Jackson took a lusty cut at Fisher's first offering, missed, and fell down, Fisher took offense that an enemy batter would swing so healthily at one of his offerings, and buzzed Jackson's head with his next pitch. Jackson retaliated by drag bunting down the first base line, knowing that Fisher would have to field the ball and putting him in Jackson's direct path to first base. "The ball rolled foul, probably as Jackson intended it should," O'Leary surmised, "and when Ray came over to the base line, Joe gave him a shove and a few remarks were passed."[12]

When the at-bat commenced, Jackson dropped a "short lob" over Kopf's head and into left field for a hit. Then Rariden took matters into his own hands. Jackson took off for second and Rariden

63

gunned him down for the first out of the inning. Felsch walked and tried to steal second, but was also erased by Rariden's right wing. Fisher caught Gandil looking at strike three to end the inning.

In terms of baseball, the action in the seventh inning was non-descript, but tempers finally boiled over and to no one's surprise Jimmy Smith was right in the middle of the fracas. According to the *New York Times*, Collins went after Smith and the two had to be separated by umpire Billy Evans. "Smith is the official goat-getter of the Reds," wrote the *Times*. "His business in life is to tarry on the base lines and tell the opposition what awful ball players they are."[13]

In the top of the eighth, Kerr set down the Reds in order again. In the bottom of the inning, Smith, who was now coaching at third, sarcastically asked Felsch when he was planning on getting a hit. Felsch was Chicago's third best hitter behind Jackson and Collins, but he'd yet to hit safely in almost three full World Series contests. Felsch responded by asking Smith what bush league he expected to be in next year.

"This so enraged Jimmy that it required the entire force of umpires and all the Cincinnati club to get Smith back to the bench," wrote Mathewson.[14]

Dolf Luque took over pitching duties for the Reds in the bottom of the eighth and began the inning with a strikeout of Leibold, and when Groh began taunting Leibold from third base, he charged down the third base line still carrying his bat. Fortunately Gleason, who was coaching at third, intercepted Leibold before he could reach the target of his ire. Collins and Weaver grounded out to end the frame.

Kerr only needed three more outs for the victory and he got them easily, getting Rath to ground out, striking out Daubert, and coaxing a game-ending grounder to Weaver, who threw out Groh at first to complete the win.

With the victory, the White Sox were back in the Series and Kerr received plaudits all around. "All that Kerr had was keen speed, a cracking curve and control that carried both where he wanted to plant them," waxed Grantland Rice.[15] "The big feature of his first championship was the rare coolness that he showed at every turn and the unending grip that he kept upon his nervous system until the last Red faded out." James O'Leary was less poetic than most. "Kerr stopped the Red sluggers with a suddenness that made their teeth rattle," he wrote.[16]

Indeed, through nine innings of work Kerr allowed only three singles, walked a batter and struck out four. He faced only 30 batters, retiring the last 15 straight.

When gambler "Sleepy Bill" Burns approached the players before Game Four with $20,000 Gandil told Burns the fix was off and they won Game Three because they felt they'd been double-crossed (in fact, Gandil drove in two of Chicago's three runs). From then on, Gandil insisted, the White Sox would be playing to win. Someone forgot to tell the Reds. They fell to Kerr again in Game Six, but took the best-of-nine series in eight games.

PART II:

1930 - 1960

MVP-lease! The Biggest World Series Flops

A lot of players who went on to win their respective league's Most Valuable Player awards showed up big in the World Series and proved that they were worthy of the honor all the way through October. But some left their regular season stats at the door and completely disappeared in the Fall Classic.

Dolph Camilli (1941)—The Dodger first baseman set new career high in homers with 34 and RBIs with 120, leading the National League in both categories on his way to MVP honors. Camilli was a very good player who led the NL in a handful of categories prior to 1941 and he received Hall of Fame support, albeit very little in four votes between 1948 and 1960.

But he failed miserably in his only World Series appearance, going 3 for 18 against the Yankees with a double, a walk, a run, an RBI and six strikeouts. Then again, the entire Dodgers roster was brutal against pinstriped pitching. Pete Reiser hit Brooklyn's only home run, and the team scored only 11 runs in five games.

Joe DiMaggio (1941)—In the dugout opposite Camilli was Hall of Famer Joe DiMaggio who won the AL MVP Award in a narrow vote

over the much more deserving Ted Williams on the strength of a
.357 batting average, 30 dingers, 125 RBIs, and an amazing 56-game
hitting streak that no one has come within sniffing distance before
or since. Joltin' Joe had already played in 19 World Series games
by the time the '41 Fall Classic rolled around and he'd been good,
hitting .304 with three homers, 12 RBIs, and 10 runs.

But 1941 against the Dodgers was a different story. He wasn't
absolutely terrible—he hit .263—but he wasn't productive either,
knocking in and scoring only one run on five singles. Bill Dickey
and Phil Rizzuto were even worse, combining to hit .139 in 36
at-bats, yet the Yankees were still able to defeat the Dodgers in five
games thanks to a pitching staff that posted a 1.80 ERA.

Joe Gordon (1942)—Twenty years prior to Mickey Mantle's postseason meltdown, Yankee second baseman Joe Gordon showed
him how it was done when the MVP batted .095 with no home runs
or RBIs, and seven strikeouts in 21 at-bats against the St. Louis
Cardinals, who easily defeated the Yanks in five games.

On the other hand, perhaps Gordon deserves a pass because he
never should have won the MVP Award to begin with. He enjoyed
an impressive season, especially for a second baseman, batting
.322 with 18 homers and 103 RBIs, but Ted Williams won the Triple
Crown with a .356 average, 36 homers, and 137 RBIs, and led the AL
in 10 offensive categories. But the writers couldn't stand Williams
and the Red Sox made the mistake of finishing second to the
Yankees in the standings.

Hal Newhouser (1945)—See page 87.

Ted Williams (1946)—After getting robbed of the AL MVP
Award in both 1941 and '42, Ted Williams finally broke through
in 1946, his first season back after serving in World War II from

1943-1945. Williams was brilliant as usual, hitting .342 with 38 home runs, 123 RBIs, a league-best and then-career-high 142 runs, and a league-leading 156 walks. He also paced the junior circuit in on-base average, slugging, OPS, OPS+, and total bases.

So what happened when he went up against the Cardinals in the 1946 Fall Classic? A whole lot of nothing. He whacked out only five hits, all singles, scored twice, and drove in only one run. He walked five times but also whiffed five times, uncharacteristic for a guy who struck out only 44 times in 672 regular season plate appearances. Alas, that would be Williams' only trip to the postseason, so he never got a chance to atone for his '46 performance.

Don Newcombe (1956)—In 1956 Dodgers ace Don Newcombe enjoyed a season for the ages, going 27-7 with a 3.06 ERA, and won both the Cy Young Award and NL MVP Award. He paced the circuit in wins, winning percentage, and WHIP at 0.989, and his 27 wins were the most in the NL since Bucky Walters turned the trick in 1939.

The 1956 Fall Classic pitted the Dodgers against the Yankees for the umpteenth time and "Dem Bums" were hoping for a repeat of the '55 Series when they beat the Bronx Bombers for the first time in six tries. Newcombe took the hill for Game Two and was shelled for six runs in 1 2/3 innings. Then he was called on to win Game Seven and another championship, but the Yankees teed off on him, especially Yogi Berra who homered twice, for five runs in three innings en route to a 9-0 slaughter.

Newk allowed 11 runs in only 4 2/3 innings for an unsightly 21.21 ERA, and finished his World Series career at 0-4 with an ERA of 8.59. Having to face the Yankees every year in the World Series can do that to you.

Mickey Mantle (1962)—Mantle won his third American League MVP Award in 1962 despite recording only 377 at-bats in 123 games. But that was because he walked a league-leading 122 times, which contributed to a league-best .486 on-base average. He also led the league in slugging, OPS, and OPS+, and belted 30 homers for the eighth straight season. Oh yeah, he also won his only Gold Glove Award.

But he was abysmal against the San Francisco Giants in the World Series, hitting .120 with no homers or runs batted in. He walked four times and scored twice, and the Yankees managed to hold on by the skin of Bobby Richardson's glove to beat the Giants in seven games, no thanks to The Mick.

Orlando Cepeda (1967)— Cardinals first baseman Orlando Cepeda enjoyed one of his best seasons in 1967 and won the NL MVP in unanimous fashion, beating out teammate Tim McCarver and Pirates legend Roberto Clemente in a landslide. Cepeda batted .325 with 25 home runs and a league-leading 111 RBIs and beat out some hitters who were arguably better, including Clemente, Cubs third baseman Ron Santo, and Hank Aaron. You could also make a case for Phillies ace Jim Bunning without getting laughed out of the room. But I digress.

Cepeda went 3 for 29 in the World Series against the Boston Red Sox with two doubles, a run and an RBI. With a slash line of .103/.103/.172 it's a good thing the Cards had Lou Brock and Bob Gibson who carried the team to victory in seven games.

Cal Ripken (1983)—The Orioles shortstop won the AL Rookie of the Year Award in 1982, then followed that up with an MVP Award in 1983 when he hit .318 with 27 four-baggers, 102 RBIs, and a league-best 120 runs scored. He also led the junior circuit in games, plate appearances, at-bats, hits, and doubles. He was excellent against the Chicago White Sox in the ALCS, reaching base eight times in four games and scoring five times.

Then things went south against the Phillies in the World Series. Ripken was decent through two games, going 2 for 7 with an RBI and a walk in a Game One loss and Game Two win. But he managed only one hit in his last 11 at-bats to finish the Series at .167 with no homers and one ribbie. Alas, 1983 would be Ripken's last chance to shine on a Fall Classic stage.

Jose Canseco (1988)—In 1988 A's slugger Jose Canseco showed the baseball world how effective performance-enhancing drugs could be when he became the first player in major league history to hit 40 homers and steal 40 bases in the same season. He led the league in four-baggers with 42 and RBIs with 124, batted a career-high .307, and received all 28 first place votes in MVP voting.

He torched Red Sox pitching in the ALCS to the tune of a .938 slugging percentage on the strength of three homers and a double in four games. But then he ran into the buzz saw that was Orel Hershiser, who held Oakland to only seven hits in two starts. Canseco launched a grand slam off Tim Belcher in the second inning of Game One before going into the witness protection program for the rest of the Series. Following his salami, Canseco went 0 for 18 as the A's got knocked out in five games.

Welcome to the Bigs, Meat

In 1939, 22-year-old rookie Gene "Junior" Thompson was outstanding for the Cincinnati Reds, going 13-5 with a 2.54 ERA in 42 games. He started 11 games, completing five of them, and tossed three shutouts. Perhaps even more impressive, though, is that Thompson allowed only six home runs in 152 1/3 innings. Among National League pitchers who tossed at least 150 innings, Thompson tied St. Louis' Mort Cooper and Brooklyn's Freddie Fitzsimmons for the league lead in fewest home runs allowed.

Five of Thompson's starts came in September and he was almost unhittable, going 5-1 with a 0.65 ERA in 11 appearances, and holding batters to a .205 average. Of the 40 hits he allowed in the month, 36 were singles and four were doubles. He allowed a home run to Hall of Fame slugger Met Ott on August 28 at the Polo Grounds, but kept the ball in the yard for the rest of the season.

So it's no wonder he was given the ball for Game Three of the 1939 Fall Classic against the vaunted and powerful New York Yankees, who scored almost 1,000 runs during the regular season and decimated the rest of the American League. Four of the Yankees' sluggers—Joe DiMaggio, Joe Gordon, Bill Dickey, and George Selkirk—finished in the top 10 in home runs.

The Yankees took the first two games of the series, beating 25-game winner Paul Derringer in Game One, and 27-game winner and NL MVP Bucky Walters in Game Two. After averaging more than six runs a game during the regular season, the Yankees scored a total of six in the first two games, the only homer coming from first baseman Babe Dahlgren, who hit 15 on the year.

Game Three was a much different story, however. "The youthful Thompson was sent into exile by a home run barrage such as only the Yankees can turn loose," wrote Irving Vaughan in the *Chicago Tribune*.[1] With Frankie Crosetti on first and one out in the first inning, rookie Charlie Keller blasted a two-run homer into the right field seats. The Reds scored a run off Lefty Gomez in the bottom of the first before he was removed from the game due to a sore back,[2] then plated two more off Bump Hadley in the second to take a brief 3-2 lead.

Thompson gave it up almost immediately. After two quick outs in the third, Thompson walked Keller, then surrendered his second round-tripper, a shot by Joe DiMaggio that cleared the center field fence and put New York back on top, 4-3. Then came the fifth. Red Rolfe singled with one out and that brought up Keller, who launched his second homer of the game. DiMaggio popped out but Bill Dickey hit a towering drive that landed almost in the same spot where Keller's smash settled.

And with that, Thompson's day was over. "When the architect put the right and center field fences on the same side of the Ohio River as home plate—instead of across the way in Kentucky," wrote John Lardner, "he was inviting massacre for his clients, and the massacre came today."[3]

Lee Grissom and Whitey Moore tossed 4 1/3 hitless innings for Cincinnati in relief, but the damage had already been done. The Yankees scored seven runs on only five hits—the four homers and Rolfe's single—then capped off a sweep when they won Game Four, 7-4, on the strength of four-baggers by Keller and Dickey.

Brother Can You Spare a Win?

Nels Potter was the epitome of a journeyman pitcher—between 1932 and 1936 the right hander bounced around the minors, hurling for five different teams and posting a record of 45-46 with a 3.77 ERA. He had one outstanding season for Lincoln of the Nebraska State League, going 17-9 with a 1.71 ERA in 1934 when he was only 22. He earned a cup of coffee with the St. Louis Cardinals in 1936 and tossed one hitless inning against Pittsburgh on April 25.

After another year in the minors, Potter made it back to the major leagues with the Philadelphia Athletics and was abysmal, going 2-12 with a

St. Louis Browns ace Nels Potter pitched beautifully in the 1944 Fall Classic, but failed to earn a win and set a record in the process.

6.47 ERA pitching mostly in relief. From 1938-1941 he went 20-39 with a 5.87 ERA with Philadelphia before the Boston Red Sox purchased him on June 30, 1941. Shirley Povich thought he'd just been unlucky in 1940. "The pitcher that's getting a tough break this year is Nelson Potter of the A's. He's pitching great ball and the A's are kicking 'em away for him. He'd win 20 games with a good ball club."[1]

Potter won two games out of the bullpen in 10 appearances with Boston, then landed in Louisville of the American Association in 1942 where he went 18-8 with a 2.60 ERA at age 30. A knee injury resulted in Potter being classified 4-F in the draft during World War II, and he took advantage of the weaker competition in 1943 after he was drafted by the St. Louis Browns in the Rule 5 draft.

The 31-year-old went 10-5 with a 2.78 ERA in 33 games, including 13 starts, then blossomed into an ace when he went 19-7 with a 2.83 ERA in 1944 to help lead the Browns to the American League pennant and a date with the Cardinals in the World Series. The Cards had won a franchise record 106 games in 1942, then followed that up with consecutive 105-49 seasons en route to three straight pennants. Meanwhile 1942 marked the Browns' first winning season since 1929, and 1944 brought them their first pennant since they began playing in the American League in 1901 as the Milwaukee Brewers. But at "only" 89-65 the Browns were heavy underdogs.

Another journeyman pitcher, 32-year-old Denny Galehouse, got the ball in Game One and scattered seven hits in a 2-1 victory over the Cards, the only Browns runs coming from a George McQuinn two-run homer in the fourth. Poor Mort Cooper surrendered only two hits for the Cards, but they came in consecutive at-bats and one happened to leave the yard.

Potter took the mound for the Browns in Game Two and was very good, giving up no earned runs in six innings, but the Cardinals pulled out a hard-fought 3-2 victory in 11 innings. One of the unearned runs came when Potter fumbled Max Lanier's bunt, then threw the ball away, committing two errors on the same play.

With the Cardinals up three games to two, Potter got the ball again in Game Six and it was more of the same—unearned runs that derailed the Browns in a 3-1 loss that gave the Cardinals their second championship in three years.

Potter tossed only 9 2/3 innings in two starts, allowing 10 hits and three walks, while fanning six. He also allowed five runs, only one of which was earned, giving him the distinction of posting the lowest World Series ERA among pitchers with at least two starts and no victories. All he had to show for his 0.93 ERA was two no-decisions and a place in a record book that few know about.

The Ultimate Fall Classic: Game Four

October 12, 1929—Chicago Cubs at Philadelphia Athletics: By 1929 the Philadelphia Athletics had come full circle. Fifteen years earlier, Connie Mack's boys had won 99 games before being swept by the "Miracle Braves" of Boston in the 1914 World Series. Only a year later, after Mack sold off, traded or lost his best players, the A's finished in last place. In fact they finished last for seven straight years before climbing back through the standings until they won another pennant in 1929 with a then-franchise best record of 104-46.

They finished 18 games ahead of the runner-up Yankees; scored just shy of six runs per game, led the league in ERA at 3.44, and boasted the best defense. Mack's infield consisted of Hall of Famers Mickey Cochrane and Jimmie Foxx, Max "Camera Eye" Bishop, who walked a league-leading 128 times, and utility man Jimmy Dykes, who posted a .950 OPS while playing three different positions. The outfield, led by Hall of Famer Al Simmons, was just as good, with "Bucketfoot Al" in left, Mule Haas in center and Bing Miller in right. Foxx and Simmons combined for 67 homers and 275 RBIs, accounting for 33% of the team's runs batted in.

The Cubs' path, meanwhile, was also littered with failure, especially in 1925 when they finished in last place, but they had remained moderately competitive since winning their last World Series in 1908. Behind skipper Joe McCarthy, the Cubs dominated the field, winning 98 games and finishing 10 1/2 games in front of the second-place Pittsburgh Pirates.

The Cubs were just as potent offensively as the A's; scoring more runs per game at 6.29. Chicago boasted Rogers Hornsby, the best hitter in the National League and that year's MVP. They also had an extremely productive outfield, led by Hall of Fame center fielder Hack Wilson, who was flanked by Riggs Stephenson in left and Hall of Famer Kiki Cuyler in right. All three drove in 100+ runs in the regular season, and the duo of Hornsby and Wilson combined for 78 homers and 308 RBIs, and, like Foxx and Simmons, accounted for a third of the team's runs batted in between them.

The Athletics fired the first salvo in Game One when surprise starter, 35-year-old, 14-year veteran Howard Ehmke, soft tossed his way to a 3-1 win, in which he struck out a then World Series record 13 batters. Game Two also went to the A's behind George Earnshaw and Lefty Grove, who combined for a 9-3 win, and Foxx and Simmons, who drove in seven runs between them.

Cubs hurler Guy Bush cut the deficit to one with a 3-1 victory in Game Three in Philadelphia, and it looked like the Bruins would even the Series at 2-2 when they went into the bottom of the seventh of Game Four with a seemingly insurmountable lead of 8-0 with staff ace Charlie Root on the mound.

But then all hell broke loose.

Mack had been unconventional with his starting pitchers the whole series, starting Ehmke in Game One, and Earnshaw in both Games Two and Three, while using his ace, Lefty Grove, in relief. Earnshaw led the staff in wins with 24 and Grove was certainly no stranger to the bullpen; in fact, he'd go on to record 55 saves during his 17-year career and led the American League in both wins and saves in 1930. But Grove was arguably the best starting pitcher in

The 1929 Philadelphia A's won at a .693 clip. Only the 1927 Yankees boasted a better single-season winning percentage to that point in American League history.

all of baseball in 1929, pacing the junior circuit in winning percentage (.769), ERA (2.81), starts (37), strikeouts (170), K/9 (5.6), and K/BB ratio (2.10), and leading all hurlers in Wins Above Replacement, Adjusted Pitching Runs, and Adjusted Pitching Wins.

In Game Two, Grove replaced an ineffective Earnshaw in the fifth and tossed 4 1/3 shutout innings, fanning six of the 16 batters he faced. Earnshaw, who averaged almost 7 1/3 innings per start during the regular season, was given the Game Three start after tossing only 4 2/3 in Game Two, and was very good, allowing only one earned run on six hits and two walks, while fanning 10, but a Jimmy Dykes error led to two unearned runs in the sixth in the Cubs' 3-1 win.

Before Game Four, Mack threw the Cubs another curveball, so to speak, when he named 46-year-old spitballer and control artist Jack Quinn as his starting hurler. On October 15, Mack finally explained that Grove was not feeling well and though it was nothing serious, the Athletics' skipper didn't feel his ace could go nine innings, which is why he'd been coming out of the bullpen.

Quinn, born Joannes Pajkos, was of Austro-Hungarian descent. He began his career with the Yankees in 1909, becoming only the second Austro-Hungarian in major league history and ended up with 247 wins and a 3.29 ERA in 23 seasons. Quinn had been solid but unspectacular in 1929, going 11-9 with a 3.97 ERA in 35 appearances.

Root went 19-6 with a 3.47 ERA in 1929 and led the league in winning percentage at .760, and he'd been very good in Game One, holding the A's to one run on three hits in seven innings, the lone tally coming courtesy of a Foxx seventh inning solo blast.

Quinn got off to a shaky start when he issued a walk to leadoff man Norm McMillan and a single to cleanup hitter Hack Wilson, but he sandwiched strikeouts of Rogers Hornsby and Kiki Cuyler around Wilson's hit to end the threat. He then navigated the next two frames largely unscathed, getting help from his shortstop Joe Boley, who made two nice plays to nip runners by an eyelash.

Root, on the other hand, was mostly masterful, setting down the A's in order in the first and second before allowing a leadoff single to Dykes in the third. Dykes went to second when Cuyler misplayed the ball, then advanced to third on a Boley sacrifice. But Root buckled down and struck out Quinn, then coaxed Bishop to ground out, and the game remained scoreless going into the fourth.

The Cubs broke through in the top of the fourth when Cuyler slashed a one-out single past Foxx, then scampered all the way around to third on a two-base error by right fielder Bing Miller. Stephenson popped out to Boley for the second out, but Charlie Grimm deposited a two-run shot over the right field wall to give the Cubs a 2-0 lead before Quinn could retire the side.

Root ran into potential trouble in the bottom of the fifth when Miller led off with a single and Wilson dropped Dykes' routine fly ball to put runners at first and second with no outs. The sun wreaked havoc on Wilson and the pitchers as it began to set behind the grandstand, and the Cubs center fielder ended up having a game he'd rather forget. But he had one spectacular play left in him when he speared Boley's long drive for the second out of the inning.

Had a double steal attempted by the A's prior to Boley's drive been successful, the A's would have plated their first run and cut the score to 2-1. But Zack Taylor threw out Miller trying to steal third, Wilson hauled in Boley's drive and Root fanned Quinn to escape the jam. Still sporting a two run lead the Cubs lit Quinn up in the sixth.

Hornsby opened the frame with a single, Wilson slapped a hit to right, then Cuyler, after two failed sacrifice attempts, drove in Hornsby with the Cubs' third straight safety. Bishop knocked down Stephenson's hit but not before Wilson scored and the Cubs had their second run of the inning and still no outs. That ended Quinn's day as Mack replaced him with lefty Rube Walberg.

Grimm laid down a beautiful sacrifice bunt that not only advanced both runners but went for a hit, and when Walberg threw the ball past Foxx and into right field in a vain attempt to get Grimm at first, Cuyler and Stephenson both scored and Grimm went all the way to third. Taylor drove in Grimm with a sacrifice fly for the Cubs' fifth run of the inning and seventh of the game, but Walberg settled down and struck out both Root and McMillan to stop the bleeding.

Root was still having his way with the A's hitters and looked invincible when he set the Mackmen down in order in the bottom of the sixth. "For six innings the bulky, stolid Charlie Root, who the fates had treated rather unkindly in the first game in Chicago, appeared riding on his way to a merited revenge," wrote John Drebinger in the *New York Times*. "Over the period he had held the mightiest of Mack sluggers in a grip of iron, allowing only three scattered hits and mowing them down as though they were men of straw."[1]

The Cubs struck again in the seventh, scoring their eighth run of the game off knuckleballer Eddie Rommel, who replaced Walberg to start the inning. Hornsby smoked a one-out triple over Haas' head, Wilson walked and Cuyler drove in Hornsby with his third hit of the game. Though he allowed three straight runners to reach base, Rommel coaxed a nifty double play off the bat of Stephenson that many insisted was a momentum shifter.

"Then came the stroke that marked the limit of Cub mastery," wrote William E. Brandt, "a double play, Dykes to Bishop to Foxx, which was a marvel of fielding speed and precision all the way through, the flashiest double play of the series so far. The Cubs were merely more than repulsed in a scoring drive. Within five minutes they were fighting furiously to block a barrage of hits."[2]

The A's broke out their hitting sticks in the bottom of the seventh and began an improbable comeback. "It was warm and sunny, but the great crowd sulked and sat in silence as Al Simmons stepped to the plate to open the Athletic half of the seventh," wrote Drebinger. "Two and three-fifths seconds later the storm broke."[3]

Simmons opened the onslaught with a massive home run to left that hit the roof of the double deck grandstand and gave the A's their first run. Foxx singled to right, then Miller dropped a blooper into center that Wilson lost in the sun. Dykes singled to score Foxx, and Boley singled to score Miller and suddenly the score was 8-3 in favor of the Cubs. Veteran first sacker "Tioga George" Burns pinch hit for Rommel and lifted an easy pop up to shortstop Woody English for the first out of the inning. Bishop singled over Root's head to score Dykes and end Root's day.

"By now the crowd had set up a terrifying din," wrote Drebinger. "The Cubs began to squirm uneasily and there was much activity on the Chicago bench as manager Joe McCarthy waved frantically to four or five pitchers warming up furiously in the bullpen. Root was taken out of the box and Arthur Nehf, veteran lefthander, took his place."[4]

Nehf, in his 15th and final season, had gone 8-5 with a career-worst 5.59 ERA in 32 appearances, more than half of which came in relief. This particular turn on the mound would prove to be his last in the majors as he wrapped up a career that saw him go 184-120 in more than 450 games.

Nehf was greeted by a routine fly ball off the bat of Haas that should have gone for the second out, but Wilson lost the ball in the sun for the third time in the contest and it got past him for a three-run homer. Legendary sportswriter Shirley Povich called it an "ordinary fly" that resulted in a "gift home run" when Wilson made a "ludicrous attempt to make the catch."[5] Wilson later explained that he didn't see Haas' fly ball until just before it hit the ground. "I stuck out my bare hand to get it, but it bounced past for a homer."[6]

The fluke round tripper pulled the A's to within one at 8-7, but they weren't finished yet. Nehf walked Cochrane and was removed from the game in favor of Sheriff Blake. Just as Nehf had been victimized by bad luck, so was Blake when Simmons' hard grounder to third skipped over McMillan's head and into left field for a single. Foxx followed with a single that plated Cochrane and the score was knotted at 8-8. "...the turmoil in the stands was now quite indescribable," Drebinger recalled. "A great gathering of staid Philadelphians had suddenly gone completely out of their minds."[7]

After only two batters, Blake was removed and Pat Malone was summoned into the game. He led the NL in wins in 1929 and 1930, going 42-19 in those two seasons, and paced the senior circuit in shutouts and strikeouts in 1929. He won 22 games in 1929 and fanned a league-leading 166 batters with a fastball that *Baseball*

Magazine's F.C. Lane claimed was one of the best in baseball.[8] But Malone also had control issues, walking a career-high 102 batters and hitting a team-high six batters.

So it was of little surprise when he drilled Miller with his first pitch to load the bases. That brought up Dykes, the 13th batter of the inning, who was 2-for-3 with an RBI and had gotten on base in all three of his plate appearances. Dykes belted a long liner to left that Stephenson barely caught. Simmons and Foxx came home on the drive and the A's were up, 10-8, and still had only one out. Malone fanned Boley and Burns to end the historic and record-setting inning.

By the time the dust settled, the Athletics had broken or tied nine World Series records, most of which had been previously held by the 1921 Giants, including most hits, most runs and most men sent to the plate in one inning. Povich called the 10-run barrage "stunning in its very force and continuity and swallowing in its completeness."[9]

With a two-run lead, Mack sent Grove to the mound to slam the door on the Cubs. He fanned two of the three batters he faced in the eighth, including pinch hitter Gabby Hartnett, then turned the trick again in the ninth, throwing only two pitches out of the strike zone. When Hornsby flied out to Miller with two down, the comeback was complete. Grove's fourth strikeout victim, Woody English, was the forty-fourth for the Cubs in the series, tying a record they'd break two days later in Game Five.

Following the historic contest Hack Wilson was in no mood to talk. "He was heartbroken and burning with pent-up rage at the same time."[10] Cubs skipper Joe McCarthy was quick to exonerate Wilson. "You can't beat the sun, can you?' he asked after the game. "They may want to blame Wilson. You can't fasten it on him. The poor kid simply lost the ball in the sun, and he didn't put the sun there."[11]

Malone started Game Five in Philadelphia and was brilliant through eight innings, allowing only two hits and a walk and striking out three while protecting a 2-0 lead. But the A's struck late again and put the World Series away with a three-run rally in the bottom of the ninth for a 3-2 walk-off victory and a 4-games-to-1 Series win.

A Returning Vet's Unusual At Bat

Some remember the 1945 World Series as the last chance the Cubs had to break a losing streak that saw them drop six Fall Classics between 1910 and 1938. Had they defeated the Detroit Tigers in 1945, Cubs fans wouldn't be nearly as neurotic as the current 107-year drought has made them. Alas, the Cubs lost in seven games and have gone 0 for their last 6 in playoff appearances.

If nothing else, the '45 Series provided some oddities. To wit:

Tigers southpaw Hal Newhouser posted back-to-back seasons that few hurlers have matched since the end of the Deadball Era when he went 29-9 with a 2.22 ERA and league-leading 187 strikeouts in 1944, then followed that by winning the pitching Triple Crown in '45 when he went 25-9 with a 1.81 ERA and 212 strikeouts. Newhouser was a beast in 1945 and paced the junior circuit in wins, ERA, starts, complete games, shutouts, innings, strikeouts, and just about everything else.

For his efforts he became only the second player to win consecutive MVP Awards after Jimmie Foxx turned the trick in 1932 and '33. Then he faced the Cubs in the World Series and he forgot he was Hal Newhouser. In Game One he gave up four runs in the first and three more in the third before he was lifted for Al Benton after only 2 2/3 innings. At that point he boasted a 23.63 ERA in World Series play.

With the Series tied at two games apiece, Newhouser got a chance to redeem himself in Game Five and he went the distance in a not very impressive 8-4 win, in which he gave up four runs on seven hits and two walks. He fanned nine, though, and reduced his ERA to 8.49. After Chicago tied the Series at three games apiece with an 8-7 win in 12 innings in Game Six, Newhouser was called upon to win the championship for the Tigers.

When the Tigers plated five runs in the top of the first off Hank Borowy, Newhouser was able to cruise to his second win of the Series, going the distance again and allowing three runs on 10 hits and a walk, while fanning 10 in a 9-3 win that dropped his ERA again to 6.10. It wasn't enough. Newhouser is the only pitcher in big league history to win at least two games in a single World Series and post an ERA above 6.00.

Borowy also set a mark that stands all by its lonesome 70 years later. He won Game One as a starter, lost Games Five and Seven as a starter, and won Game Six with four innings of scoreless relief, making him the only pitcher to go 2-2 in a World Series.

But the oddest moment might have come in the bottom of the ninth inning of Game Seven when Cubs catcher Clyde McCullough pinch hit for pitcher Hank Wyse with a runner on first and no outs. The right handed hitting backstop was a career .245 hitter who hit a career-high nine home runs in 1941, and manager Charlie Grimm was grasping at straws. Wyse had batted only .168 that year and had a career average of .153 to that point, so McCullough looked like a much better option.

But he fanned against Newhouser, who then retired Stan Hack and Don Johnson to cap off the game and championship. What made McCullough's at-bat odd is that he had spent the entire 1944 and '45 seasons in the Navy and hadn't batted in a major league game since September 30, 1943. McCullough is the only player to bat in a World Series after having no plate appearances in the regular season.[1]

Hitless Wonders: An All-Time 0-fer Lineup

Catcher—Billy Sullivan (1906): Sullivan actually spent most of his career with a team known as "The Hitless Wonders," so this comes as no surprise. The White Sox backstop batted only .214 in 1906, and that was his highest mark from 1905-1910 when he combined to hit .191 in 607 games.

Needless to say, Sullivan wasn't in the lineup because of his bat. And he proved it in the 1906 Fall Classic when he went 0 for 21 with nine strikeouts. In Sullivan's defense he was facing a Chicago Cubs pitching staff that allowed only 2.46 runs per game during the regular season and boasted the second best ERA in modern day history at a miniscule 1.75. As a team, the White Sox batted only .198 but still managed to win the World Series in six games, mostly because the Cubs' batters were even worse.

First Base—Gil Hodges (1952): At first glance, 1952 doesn't jump out as one of Hodges' better years—he batted only .254 and fanned 90 times—but his 142 OPS+ was the best of his career. He belted 32 homers for the Brooklyn Dodgers, drove in 102 runs, and walked a career-high 107 times. But the 28-year-old slugger couldn't buy a hit in the 1952 Fall Classic and went 0 for 21, albeit with five walks.

Most fans would have started booing at some point, but Brooklyn fans continued to cheer for him throughout the Series. And many of them prayed for him. "Hodges was a religious man, a practicing catholic, and from pulpits in Flatbush, Canarsie, South Brooklyn, and Williamsburg, congregations implored the Lord to aid Gil Hodges," wrote Peter Golenbock in *Bums: An Oral History of the Brooklyn Dodgers*.[1] The Lord finally answered...in the 1953 Series when Hodges batted .364 with a homer against the Yankees.

Second Base—Placido Polanco (2006): Few players went from the penthouse to the outhouse faster than Polanco in the 2006 post-season. After hitting .295 for the Detroit Tigers during the regular season, Polanco was unstoppable in the Division and League Championship Series, going 16 for 34 (.471) against the Yankees and A's, and helping the Tigers reach the World Series for the first time since 1984. He was so good in the ALCS, batting .529 in four games, that he was named ALCS MVP.

Then the World Series began and he suddenly forgot how to hit. In five games against the St. Louis Cardinals, Polanco went 0 for 17. He reached base twice after being hit by a Josh Kinney pitch in Game Two and drawing a walk in his final at-bat of the Series, but the latter preceded a Brandon Inge strikeout that ended the game and Series for the Tigers.

Third Base—Flea Clifton (1935): Herman Earl Clifton played only 85 major league games in four years with Detroit mainly because he couldn't hit or field. On the other hand he went 5 for 7 in stolen base attempts, so maybe he could run a little. But I digress. He enjoyed his best season in 1935 when he batted .255 in 43 games while playing an underwhelming third base that wasn't going to make Tigers fans forget Ossie Vitt anytime soon. For the first two games of the '35 Fall Classic, Clifton was firmly ensconced on Detroit's bench while his teammates split the first two games at home.

Then the unthinkable happened—slugging first baseman Hank Greenberg, who would go on to win the league's MVP Award that year, broke his wrist while sliding into home in the seventh inning of Game Two. That gave Clifton his moment in the sun. Regular third baseman Marv Owen was shifted to first and Flea was penciled in at the hot corner where he more than lived up to his name, going 0 for 16 with two walks and an error. Meanwhile Owen went 1 for 15 after replacing Greenberg at first, giving the Tigers a corner infield tandem that batted .032 in the Series.

Shortstop—Dal Maxvill (1968): Few batters could hit in 1968 and Maxvill was no exception. He batted .253 with only 14 extra-base hits in 151 games for the Cardinals and that was his best season in a 14-year career. He batted only .115 in four World Series and was never worse than in '68 when he went 0 for 22 against the Tigers.

Versus Tigers ace Denny McLain and World Series hero Mickey Lolich, the righty-swinging shortstop went 0 for 14 with four strikeouts and a walk. Including the LCS, Maxvill played in six postseason series in his career and had more walks (9) than hits (8). How any pitcher could walk someone with a career .115 postseason average is anybody's guess.

Left Field—Jimmy Sheckard (1906): Unlike Billy Sullivan, Sheckard was a good offensive player who led his circuit in 11 categories during his 17-year career, including walks, stolen bases, and sacrifice hits twice each. But Sheckard wasn't just a light-hitting speedster, having also paced the National League in triples and slugging in 1901, and home runs in 1903.

Legend has it that Sheckard predicted he'd hit .400 against the White Sox's pitching staff in the 1906 World Series, but he was clearly overmatched, going 0 for 21 with two walks. Even when the Cubs' bats broke out in a 7-1 romp in Game Two during which the Cubs had 10 hits, only Sheckard and pitcher Ed Reulbach went hitless. To make matters worse, Sheckard hit only one ball out of the infield during the entire Series.

Center Field—Carl Reynolds (1938): It's almost unfair to include Reynolds on this squad since he had "only" 12 hitless at-bats for the Cubs against the Yankees in the 1938 World Series. But he was the worst among qualifying center fielders (Wally Berger played mostly left field when he went 0 for 15 in 1939). Reynolds made his mark with the post-Black Sox Scandal White Sox and enjoyed his best season in 1930 when he batted .359 with 22 home runs and 104 RBIs.

In 1938 the 35-year-old was still a productive hitter, albeit for the crosstown Cubs, and was going into the World Series on a hot streak, having batted .331 over his final 30 regular season games. But he couldn't solve New York's pitching and joined the ranks of players who failed to record a hit in the Fall Classic.

Right Field—Red Murray (1911): In 1911 the Giants right fielder set a career-high with a .781 OPS and was only two years removed from leading the National League in homers with seven. He hit only three round trippers but smacked a career-best 27 doubles, tied a then-career high in triples with 15, and stole 48 bases. Murray was one of John McGraw's better regulars and batted cleanup for the Giants, but he completely disappeared during the World Series.

Murray went 0 for 21, including 0 for 12 with men on base, and committed three errors in the field. He was especially bad in Game Five, going 0 for 5 with three whiffs, and stranded four men in scoring position, although the Giants won 4-3 in 10 innings thanks to Fred Merkle's walk-off sacrifice fly.

It's hard to blame Murray for the Giants' World Series loss to the Philadelphia Athletics, though. New York batted only .175 as a team and scored 13 runs in six games thanks to the brilliant pitching of Chief Bender, Jack Coombs, and Eddie Plank, who pitched to a combined 1.29 ERA. But he certainly didn't help.

Mickey Grasso: POW at the Plate

Newton Grasso was a fairly nondescript catcher who finished his seven-year big league career with a .226 average and only five home runs in 322 games with the New York Giants, Washington Senators, and Cleveland Indians. But he was extremely popular, especially as a member of the Pacific Coast League's Seattle Rainiers with whom he boasted a fan club of 5,000 adoring members.

Grasso earned the nickname "Mickey" thanks to his uncanny resemblance to Hall of Fame backstop Mickey Cochrane, although he'd never come close to replicating Cochrane's accomplishments. Still, Grasso was well-liked wherever he went. The New Jersey native began his career at age 21 with Trenton of the Interstate League and batted .234 in 52 games. But like many ballplayers of that era, he joined the service after the bombing of Pearl Harbor and went off to war.

Grasso enlisted in the army and was stationed in North Africa with the 34th Infantry Division, but was captured by Erwin Rommel's army in early 1943. Grasso spent the next two years in Stalag 111B in Furstenberg, Germany and was severely beaten after each of his failed escape attempts. Finally, he escaped in April 1945 as the Russian army was closing in on the Nazi camp. He recovered from a 60-pound weight loss and signed with the Giants' Triple-A affiliate in Jersey City where he spent most of the 1946 season and batted .228 with 13 homers.

He made his major league debut with the Giants on September 18, 1946 and went 0 for 4 with a strikeout against the Chicago Cubs. He played only seven games that year before heading back to the minors where he spent the next three seasons before reappearing in the bigs with the Senators in 1950. After four seasons with Washington with whom he batted .228 in 303 games, Grasso was traded to the Indians prior to the 1954 season.

He broke his left ankle in spring training and appeared in only four games for the Indians, going 2 for 6 with a homer and an RBI, but he entered Game One of the 1954 World Series in the bottom of the 10th and was behind the plate when Dusty Rhodes belted a walk-off three-run homer off Bob Lemon to give the Giants a 5-2 win en route to a four-game sweep.

When Grasso entered the game, he became the first and only former prisoner of war to appear in a World Series game.[1]

Here's Your Hat...

If Art Ditmar's selection as the Yankees' Game One starter in the 1960 World Series against the Pittsburgh Pirates wasn't controversial before the game, it certainly was after. Few could understand why Casey Stengel would go with Ditmar rather than Whitey Ford, a man with 12 career World Series starts under his belt, a 5-4 record and 2.81 ERA in World Series play, and four championship rings.

Ditmar led the Yankees with 15 wins and 200 innings, and boasted the best ERA in the rotation at 3.06,[1] but had never started a World Series game in his seven-year career, although he was very effective in relief in both the 1957 and '58 Fall Classics. Legend has it that Stengel wanted to save Ford for Game Three at Yankee Stadium because he thought the dimensions were more favorable to the southpaw than the ones at Forbes Field. He also thought the hard infield at Forbes would hurt a ground ball pitcher like Ford and result in more balls getting through for base hits.[2]

That made no sense to Yankees hurler Ralph Terry, who wondered why Stengel would go with a sinkerball pitcher like Ditmar if he was, in fact, worried about Pittsburgh's infield. He also reasoned that Ford could start only one of the three games at Yankee Stadium so why not start him in Game One at Forbes, then give him the ball again in Game Four at the Stadium?[3]

Casey Stengel will always be second guessed for starting Art Ditmar
(left) in Game One of the 1960 World Series instead of Whitey Ford.
Bobby Shantz is on the right.

When asked why he chose Ditmar over Ford, Stengel said, "I
decided I better pick him because some times this year he won the
first game of important series we played." He also claimed that
his "second-stringers" had been pitching better than his top-line
starters over the season's final three weeks.[4]

He was right. Ditmar and Ford, Stengel's aces, combined to go
4-2 with ERAs of 3.52 and 4.10, respectively, in their final five starts
of the season. Meanwhile, Ralph Terry (3-0, 0.93), Bill Stafford
(1.69) and Bob Turley (2-0, 1.89) were all hot going into the World
Series. Yankees pitching coach Eddie Lopat wanted the 21-year-
old Stafford to get the ball in Game One, but coaches Ralph Houk
and Frankie Crosetti thought it unwise to kick off the Series with a
rookie on the mound.[5]

Houk and Crosetti won the argument and Stengel went with
Ditmar, who lasted all of five batters despite being handed a 1-0
lead when Roger Maris slammed a drive into the right field seats

in the top of the first. Bill Virdon led off for the Pirates and drew a walk. The next play caused confusion on the field and in newspapers the following day depending on the perspective. Virdon took off for second on what was described as a delayed steal [6] and landed on third when Yogi Berra fired the ball into center field.

In Berra's defense, shortstop Tony Kubek was supposed to cover second on the play, but was late getting there. With right-handed batter Dick Groat up, the Yanks figured he'd try to go to right field and left second baseman Bobby Richardson in position just in case. Harold Kaese reported that Virdon received no signal from Murtaugh and decided to go on his own.[7] Groat confirmed as much. "I was surprised to see him going, and wondered if we had messed up a hit-and-run sign."[8]

After the game, the Yankees insisted the "delayed steal" was a cover-up because Virdon had screwed up the signs and was embarrassed to admit it.[9] Others thought the hit-and-run was on but Groat decided to take the pitch to deke the Yankees out of their shoes. Regardless, the Pirates caught the Yankees off guard and had a runner on third with no one out. He didn't stay there long.

Groat doubled to right to tie the game, and that brought Stengel to the mound for a chat with Ditmar. "Casey's remarks were not recorded," wrote the *Los Angeles Times*. "But maybe Ditmar wasn't listening anyway...".[10] Bob Skinner poked a single into center field to plate Groat, then stole second and would have gone to third had Kubek not speared Berra's throw behind the bag. Again, neither middle infielder was at second in time to make a play. It hardly mattered, though, when Roberto Clemente singled in Skinner to give Pittsburgh a 3-1 lead. And, with that, Ditmar's day was over.

Jim Coates and Duke Maas pitched the next 4 1/3 innings and allowed three more runs between them before Ryne Duren finished the game for the Yankees with two scoreless innings. Vern Law was mostly excellent for the Pirates, surrendering only one run in his last six innings after giving up Maris' homer in the first, but he needed some help from Virdon, who pulled down a long drive off Berra's bat that killed a fourth inning rally. Roy Face allowed a two-run homer to Elston Howard in the top of the ninth, but was able to close out a 6-4 Pirates victory.

After the game, Ditmar said with a grin, "There was nothing wrong with me—I just wasn't getting 'em out."[11] Stengel wasn't exactly thrilled. "I'd have to say our first pitcher (Art Ditmar) pitched bad," Casey told reporters after the game. "You certainly couldn't say he pitched good."[12] Bill Lee of the *Hartford Courant* was a little kinder in his assessment of Ditmar. "It would not be fair to say that he did not get anybody out," he wrote. "He did. He got one man out."[13]

The Yankees won Games Two and Three behind Bob Turley and Whitey Ford, who allowed only three runs between them—Ford tossed a complete-game four-hit shutout—while their teammates pummeled Pirates pitching for 26 runs on 35 hits. Pittsburgh tied the Series at two games apiece with a 3-2 win in Game Four behind another solid outing by Vern Law and 2 2/3 hitless innings by Face.

Stengel had a major decision to make for Game Five—give Art Ditmar another start or go with young rookie Bill Stafford. According to most accounts, "The Old Perfessor" had settled on Stafford[14] but had a change of heart the morning of the fifth game. "Ditmar's an experienced pitcher, who won 15 games in the American League this year," the 70-year-old skipper explained. "He pitched only a half-game in Pittsburgh last week," he continued, obviously forgetting that Ditmar pitched only a third of an inning, "and he wasn't tired."[15]

What's Your Hurry?

Ditmar barely lasted as long in Game Five as he had in Game One, although had he received help from teammates and a sliver of confidence from Stengel it might have been a different story. Unlike in his previous appearance, he retired the side in order in the top of the first, but things began to unravel quickly in the second. Slugger Dick Stuart, who went into the game hitting only .167 in 12 World Series at-bats, led off with a single, but was erased from the base paths by a Gino Cimoli force out at second. Smoky Burgess doubled to right to put Pirates on second and third, and that's when the wheels fell off; Don Hoak grounded to shortstop Tony Kubek, who tried to get Burgess going to third, but Gil McDougald dropped the ball while trying to make the tag and everyone was safe.

Cimoli scored on the play to give Pittsburgh a 1-0 lead and Hoak moved to second on the error. "Tony made a perfect throw," McDougald told reporters after the game. "I dropped the ball because I was in too much of a hurry to tag the runner."[16] Bill Mazeroski followed with a grounder that bounced over McDougald's head for a double and was described as a "groundkeeper's hop" when it ricocheted into left field and plated two more runs for a 3-0 Pirates lead.

And that was that for Ditmar. "Stengel's confidence in Ditmar had by this time been completely shattered," wrote Ed Rumill in *The Christian Science Monitor*, "making all of us wonder how the right-hander ever got to work the opener of this classic, then asked to start again, Oct. 10."[17] But Stengel had Ditmar's back. "There was nothing wrong with starting Ditmar or his pitching," Casey insisted. "The Pirates didn't overpower or overwhelm him. They were bouncing balls through infields and over heads, and our fielders didn't field too good behind him, either."[18]

Stengel tabbed Luis Arroyo to finish the inning before finally calling on Stafford, who shut the Pirates down for five innings, allowing only three hits before making way for Ryne Duren in the eighth. "I guess I should have started Stafford instead of Ditmar," Stengel admitted after the game. "Stafford showed me that he is an established big league pitcher."[19] But he didn't blame Ditmar for the loss. "I can't knock Ditmar. Burgess got the only real hit off him, but that's the way it goes in this game. Everywhere Ditmar pitched they seemed to hit it into the hole."[20]

The 5-2 loss put the Yankees in a 3-2 hole, which they overcame with another blowout win in Game Six, a 12-0 whitewash that featured 17 more New York hits and a seven-hit shutout by Whitey Ford, his second of the Series. Of course that set up one of the most memorable and dramatic games in World Series history and cemented Bill Mazeroski's legacy when his homer in the bottom of the ninth of Game Seven off Ralph Terry gave the Pirates their first championship since 1925.

As of this writing no pitcher has ever pitched fewer innings in multiple starts than Art Ditmar, who tossed only 1 2/3 in two starts and faced only 13 batters.

The Ultimate Fall Classic: Game Five

October 8, 1956—Brooklyn Dodgers at New York Yankees: In 1956 the Yankees and Dodgers squared off for the seventh time in October and sixth time in 10 years. The Bronx Bombers took the first five meetings, two of which went seven games, before "Dem Bums" finally broke through in 1955 for their first championship in the modern era. From 1920, Babe Ruth's first season in pinstripes, to 1955, the Yankees won 62% of their regular season games, 21 American League pennants and 16 World Series titles. From 1916, Brooklyn's first appearance in a modern era World Series, until 1955, the Dodgers won more than 53% of their regular season games, eight National League pennants and the aforementioned defeat of the Yankees in the '55 Fall Classic.

Nineteen-fifty-six proved to be another banner year for both clubs and it was fitting that they'd meet again in the postseason, considering they finished either first or second in their respective leagues in hitting, pitching and fielding efficiency, the only two teams to do so. New York, led by triple crown winner and AL MVP Mickey Mantle, scored a league-high 5.56 runs per game, almost a full run better than average. The Dodgers, led by center fielder Duke Snider, plated 4.68 runs per game.

The Yankees, paced by southpaw Whitey Ford (19-6 with a 2.47 ERA), also had the edge in pitching—they finished second to

Cleveland in ERA at 3.63 and boasted a slightly higher ERA than the Dodgers' 3.57, but were more than a half run better than league average, whereas Brooklyn, led by Don Newcombe (27-7, 3.06) was only .2 runs better than league average. But the Dodgers were the best defensive team in baseball, leading the majors in defensive efficiency at .730, while the Yankees finished second in the AL at .713, and seventh in the majors.

From 1947-1955, the clubs met five times in the World Series and four of them had gone to 2-2 heading into the fifth game, so it was no surprise when the '56 Series was knotted at two games apiece going into Game Five. What was a surprise, however, was that Yankees manager Casey Stengel was going to go with 27-year-old 11-game winner Don Larsen in what was a pivotal tilt. Larsen had been brilliant in September, going 4-0 and allowing only two earned runs in his final 34 2/3 innings for a microscopic 0.52 ERA, but couldn't get out of the second inning of Game Two when he allowed four runs on four walks and a hit before being replaced by Johnny Kucks.

All four runs were unearned thanks to an error by first baseman Joe Collins, but the meltdown by the Yankees pitching staff—Stengel used three pitchers in the second alone and seven in the game—erased a six-run advantage they held going into the top of the second en route to a 13-8 loss. It appeared to be a crushing blow to the Yankees, who'd also lost Game One, 6-3, when ace Whitey Ford was pummeled for five runs on six hits in only three innings.

Ford rebounded and won Game Three at Yankee Stadium, then Tom Sturdivant, a 26-year-old in his sophomore season, earned a 6-2 win in Game Four to knot the series at two games apiece. Dodgers skipper Walter Alston tabbed Sal "The Barber" Maglie for Game Five. Stengel countered with Larsen, a decision that "fooled a lot of smart people," wrote Frank Finch of the *Los Angeles Times*. "Most felt that Bullet Bob Turley or Johnny Kuck [sic] would get the nod." Larsen went 11-5 with a 3.26 ERA and boasted a terrific fastball, rated one of the best by *The Sporting News*, a slider, and a slow curve, but had the least success against the Dodgers in the postseason, pitching to an 11.25 ERA in his only start in Game Four of the '55 Fall Classic.

"Larsen was a Jeckyl and Hyde pitcher who alternated steady performances with ones where he didn't throw a strike for a week," explained the introduction to Larsen's book, *The Perfect Yankee: The Incredible Story of the Greatest Miracle in Baseball*.[1] But, with only a few games left in the '56 campaign, Larsen adopted a no-windup delivery that proved effective in his last two regular season starts. "This idea of pitching without a windup came to me about 10 minutes before I went out to face the Red Sox about two weeks ago," the hurler explained. "So I went out and tried it and I beat them, 2-1, on a four-hitter."[2] Six days later he held Boston to no runs on three hits in seven innings.

According to legend, sometime during the night Larsen told Richman that he was going to toss a no-hitter, then gave him a dollar to donate to his synagogue for good luck. Larsen insists that he didn't say he "would" throw a no-hitter, he said he "might." Either way, he was right.[3]

Larsen had no idea he'd be starting until he arrived at the Yankees' clubhouse and found the warm-up ball in his shoe, left there by coach Frankie Crosetti. When the big righthander took the mound in the top of the first, he was met by almost 65,000 fans anxious to see who would climb into the driver's seat heading into Game Six. Junior Gilliam led off and struck out looking. Pee Wee Reese took the count to three balls and two strikes before fanning on a called third strike. It would be the only time Larsen would get to three balls on a batter the rest of the way. Duke Snider lined out to right field to end the inning.

"In the first inning Gilliam and Reese set the negative tempo by window shopping Larsen's throws," wrote Bugs Baer. "From then on the Bums took it like they were batting with spoons."[4]

Maglie was equally effective, retiring the side in order. Larsen almost ran into trouble in the second when Jackie Robinson led off with a smash that caromed off third baseman Andy Carey's glove, but shortstop Gil McDougald snagged the rebound and tossed Robinson out by a step. Gil Hodges fanned on four pitches, then Sandy Amoros popped out to second.

Again, Maglie matched Larsen pitch for pitch and retired the side in order, then Larsen retired the Dodgers in the top of the third on only seven pitches. And the beat went on—the 39-year-old Maglie mastered the Yankees again in the bottom of the third, retiring McDougald, Carey, and Larsen on a grounder to third and two pop outs to Roy Campanella, then Larsen set down the Dodgers in the fourth on seven more pitches, one of which was a long foul into the lower deck of the right field stands by Duke Snider two pitches before striking out.

Going into the bottom of the fourth, 21 batters had stepped to the plate and the closest anyone had come to a hit was Robinson. "The 64,519 spectators had already started buzzing that a double no-hitter might be in the making..." wrote Edward Prell in the *Chicago Tribune*[5]. Interestingly, Maglie had just thrown a no-hitter on September 25 against the Phillies in his second-to-last start of the season. The closest Larsen had ever come to a no-no was on May 16, 1954 when the then Baltimore Orioles hurler held the Yankees hitless for 7 2/3 innings before surrendering his first safety.

Prior to the '56 World Series, Maglie had faced the Yankees in postseason play once before, in 1951 when he was rocked in Game Four and lost to Allie Reynolds, 6-2. Hall of Fame center fielder Joe DiMaggio took him deep in the fifth to ice the game and effectively end Maglie's day. But this time he was in full control, at least through the first 11 Yankee hitters.

Hank Bauer led off the fourth with a grounder to third and Collins struck out looking, bringing Mickey Mantle to the plate with two down and nobody on. The man who would eventually replace DiMaggio in the Yankee outfield treated Maglie the same as his predecessor had and ripped a line drive into the right field seats to give the Yankees a 1-0 lead that Larsen would never relinquish. "Mantle got hold of a souvenir ball and gave it the long autograph," wrote Bugs Baer.[6]

Yogi Berra lined out to Snider, who made a "brilliant diving gloved-hand catch" to end the inning and bring Larsen out for the fifth. Robinson led off the frame and slammed a drive to deep right field where it was corralled by Bauer. Hodges belted a shot to deep left-center, but Mantle got on his horse and made a running back-handed grab of the drive for out number two. Then Amoros smacked a 1-1 offering into the lower deck of the right field seats, but it went just foul for a loud strike two. Two pitches later, he bounced out to Billy Martin to end the inning.

The Yankees appeared to have something going in the bottom of the fifth when Enos Slaughter walked to lead off the inning, but Martin's bunt resulted in a force out, Maglie to Reese, then the Dodgers' captain made a sensational play on a drive off the bat of McDougald to end the threat. McDougald's liner appeared to be headed for left-center field, "but the ball never cleared Reese, who leaped in the air, deflected the ball with his glove, then caught it," wrote John Drebinger in the *New York Times*. "Martin, certain the drive was a hit, had gone too far off first to get back and was doubled off the bag."[7]

Larsen continued his efficient domination in the sixth, using only three pitches to set down Carl Furillo and Campanella on consecutive pop flies to Martin. The toughest batter of the inning proved to be Maglie, who battled Larsen for six pitches before finally fanning on the seventh to end the frame. Maglie's luck ran out in the bottom of the sixth when he surrendered a hit to Carey, a sacrifice bunt by Larsen and a hit to Bauer that brought Carey home with New York's second run. Collins singled and Bauer advanced to third to put runners on the corners with only one out and Mantle coming to the plate.

Alston made a trip to the mound to talk to Maglie, Reese and Gilliam. "When I walked out to the mound in the sixth...I just wanted to find out how he felt, and as soon as he told me he was all right I didn't hesitate to leave him in," the Dodgers pilot explained after the game. "I wanted to talk to Pee Wee Reese and Junior Gilliam to set up a double play situation, too."[8] Mantle did, in fact, hit into a double play. In what was described as a "rather freakish" twin killing by Drebinger, Mantle bounced sharply to Hodges, who fielded the ball, stepped on first, then fired to Campanella to nail Bauer in a rundown between third and home.[9]

Larsen set the Dodgers down again in the seventh, then tempted fate and started talking about what he might accomplish with two more perfect innings.

"Still, it was not until after Larsen had set down the Dodgers in the seventh inning that he realized what might happen," wrote Kostya Kennedy in *Sports Illustrated*. "Sitting in the dugout, a lit cigarette in his hand, he stared out at the scoreboard and saw the string of zeros. 'Hey, Mick,' said Larsen to Mantle, who was beside him. 'Look at that. Two more innings. Wouldn't it be something.'[10]

"Mantle stood and walked away without saying a word. At that point superstition took over. No one dared mention the no-hitter or even talk to Larsen. The dugout, usually full of banter, fell suddenly silent. 'It was lonely in there those last two innings,' Larsen recalls. 'The only time I felt comfortable was when I was on the mound.'"[11]

The rest of the ballpark was also well aware of what they were witnessing. "Somewhere in the middle of the game the crowd seemed to get a mass realization of the wonders that were being unfolded," wrote Arthur Daley of the *New York Times*. "Tension kept mounting until it was as brittle as an electric light bulb. The slightest jounce and the dang thing might explode."[12]

Maglie ran into a bit of trouble in the bottom of the seventh when he surrendered a two-out hit to Martin and a walk to McDougald, but he coaxed Carey to ground to Reese, who flipped the ball to Gilliam at second for the force. Larsen continued his three-up, three-down pace in the eighth and retired Robinson, Hodges and Amoros on a grounder back to the mound, a liner to third and a deep fly to center.

Larsen led off the bottom of the eighth and received a rousing ovation from the home crowd. "When Larsen came to bat in the eighth the vast old stadium shook with the thunder of acclaim, and torn programs fluttered down from on high in a blizzard reserved locally for visiting potentates and early swimmers of the English Channel," waxed Bob Considine.[13]

As if to remind everyone how fantastic he'd been throughout the contest as well, Maglie struck out the side in the bottom of the eighth, earning a nice ovation from the crowd as he headed back to the dugout. But he didn't stop there. "When Sal Maglie finished striking out three Yankees in the eighth inning...he went directly down the steps and through the Dodgers' dugout without pausing," wrote Roscoe McGowen. "Looking neither to the right nor the left Sal sat down on the low wall that borders the runway, clasped his hands and leaned over with bowed head...Had the Barber been praying?"[14]

According to Povich, the Yankees eighth-inning strikeout victims "weren't caring much or even bothering to bark at some of the strike calls Sal Maglie was getting. They were un-naturally docile. Yankee runs weren't important now."[15] The big Yankee right hander came out for the top of the ninth and a shot at immortality. "Out from the stands swept a low murmur of excitement," wrote Daley, "almost like surf rumbling against a distant shore."[16]

All Larsen had to do was retire the next three batters and he'd become the first pitcher to toss a no-hitter in World Series play. But this wasn't any no-hitter; it was a perfect game. Furillo led off the top of the ninth. "One could have heard a dollar bill drop in the huge arena as Carl Furillo got up as the first Dodger batter in the ninth," recounted Drebinger.[17] The right-handed hitting, strong-armed Pennsylvania native gave Larsen arguably his toughest battle of the contest when he fouled off four of the first five pitches he saw before rapping a high fly to Bauer in right. "A gush of relief spilled from the crowded stands," wrote Bob Considine.[18]

Two outs to go.

"Larsen took his cap off and shook his head, apparently to dislodge any cold sweat on his brow," wrote Daley.[19] The pitcher's next hurdle was hard-hitting catcher Roy Campanella. "Larsen, wet with sweat though it was a pleasantly cool afternoon, confronted the Dodger catcher with great deliberation," wrote Considine.[20] Campy belted a long foul to left, then hit a dribbler to Martin at second for out number two. "Brash Billy the Kid scooped the ball up and aimed carefully as he pegged to Joe Collins," wrote Daley. "The surf no longer was pounding on a distant shore. It was close at hand, a mighty roar."[21]

One out to go.

Maglie was due up, but Alston summoned left-handed hitting 34-year-old veteran Dale Mitchell to hit for the hard-luck Dodgers hurler. Mitchell, in his 11th and final season, was a career .312 hitter who fanned only 119 times in just shy of 4,000 career at-bats. He struck out only 17 times per 162 games and boasted a career on-base percentage of .368. "Dale is a clean-swinging, clean-living professional who is kind to children and dogs," wrote Considine of Mitchell. "But no man living was 'for' him as he stood up there, the last human barricade between Larsen and immortality."[22]

"Larsen took off his cap, looked around at his deployed teammates, jiggled the ball in his glove, and wiped his right hand on his

Yankees catcher Yogi Berra embraces Don Larsen after Larsen fanned Dale Mitchell to cap off his perfect game in Game Five of the 1956 World Series.

striped flannels before delivering a pitch which was outside" wrote Ed Prell.[23] Larsen evened the count at 1-1 with a called strike, then jumped ahead 1-2 when Mitchell swung at and missed his third offering. "Larsen again jerked off his cap," wrote Prell, "nervously brushed the back of his neck with it, reached down for the resin bag—and pitched."[24] Mitchell fouled the ball off to the left and into the crowd. "Don gently kicked the dirt around the rubber," Prell continued, "again went to the resin bag and then into his pitching position. He drew back, the arm flashed forward, and Mitchell stood there as tho [sic] transfixed."[25]

Mitchell started to offer at the pitch but thought it was off the plate and checked his swing. "That ball was this far outside,"

Mitchell explained after the game, holding his hands about a foot apart.[26] Perhaps caught up in the moment, home plate umpire Babe Pinelli rung him up anyway to seal the perfect game. "It was a fat pitch," Pinelli countered. "No hitter will see a much better strike."[27] Interestingly, it would prove to be Mitchell's last career plate appearance and Pinelli's last home plate assignment, the arbiter having decided to retire after the season.

Yankee Stadium erupted. "Those staid Yankee fans went nuts in an unrestrained ovation that was far more indigenous to Ebbets Field," wrote Daley.[28] Yogi Berra raced toward Larsen, jumped on the pitcher and wrapped his arms and legs around him in a congratulatory embrace.

One newspaper joked that the closest a Dodger got to first base was coach Jake Pitler.

Reliever Clem Labine started Game Six for the Dodgers and was brilliant, shutting out the Yankees for 10 innings to win, 1-0, beating hard-luck loser Bob Turley, who tossed 9 2/3 shutout innings before surrendering the winning run. But the Yankees secured yet another championship with a 9-0 Game Seven drubbing at Ebbets Field behind the three-hit pitching of Johnny Kucks. Larsen owned the only no-hitter in postseason history for 54 years before Roy Halladay turned the trick against the Cincinnati Reds in Game One of the 2010 NLDS, and is still the only pitcher to hurl a perfect game in the postseason.

PART III:

1960 - PRESENT

Mind-Numbing Numbers:
The Oddest World Series Stat Lines

Nick Maddox vs. Ed Summers (1909 World Series, Game Three):
On October 11, 1909 with the Series between the Pirates and Tigers tied at one game apiece, 13-game winner Maddox went to battle against 19-game winner "Kickapoo Ed" Summers. Pittsburgh jumped all over Summers and plated five runs in the first inning, sending Summers to an early exit. He lasted only a third of an inning, but thanks to a handful of errors behind him, he was credited with no earned runs allowed.

Maddox tossed the whole game and allowed six runs in an 8-6 victory, but two Bill Abstein errors behind him resulted in five unearned runs. So the starters combined to allow 11 runs between them, but only one was earned. And of the 14 runs that crossed the plate in the game, only three were earned thanks to seven errors, five of which were committed by the Tigers.

Lefty Tyler (1918): Tyler started three games against the Boston Red Sox in the 1918 Fall Classic and went 1-1 with a nifty 1.17 ERA in a losing cause. But what makes his stat line so bizarre is that he walked 11 batters in 23 innings while fanning only four. Others with at least 20 innings pitched have walked at least 10 batters in a single Series, but Tyler was the only one who failed to whiff as many as five batters. In fact, the next closest member of the 10-walk club is Art Nehf, who walked 13 Yankees in 1921, but also fanned eight. The others on the list all struck out more batters than they walked.

Jesse Barnes (1921): Barnes was a seven-year veteran in 1921 and his career had been a rollercoaster ride to that point—He led the National League in losses in 1917 when he fell 21 times for the Boston Braves, then paced the league with 25 wins in 1919 for the New York Giants. Five years later he'd lead the league in losses again with 20 for the Braves, while also finishing first in shutouts. If nothing else, Barnes kept things interesting.

One thing Barnes was never good at was striking out batters, but you would never guess based on his performance against the vaunted Yankees in 1921. Barnes fanned only 56 batters in 258 2/3 innings in the regular season for an anemic 1.9 whiffs per nine innings. Considering Walter Johnson was blowing away almost five batters a game and the average hurler was around 2.68, it's obvious Barnes wasn't in the same league.

But he did his best "Big Train" impersonation when he struck out 18 Yankees in 16 1/3 relief innings to help the Giants win the 1921 World Series in seven games. His most impressive performance came in Game Six when he relieved Fred Toney with two outs in the first inning, then proceeded to toy with the Yankees for the next 8 1/3 innings, allowing only two runs on four hits and striking out 10.

His 9.9 whiffs per nine innings was well above his season mark, and to prove it wasn't a fluke he struck out six more Yankees in 10 innings the following year and finished his World Series career with a K/9 IP mark of 8.2.

Mike Gazella (1926, Game Five): Gazella was a little used third baseman on the Murderer's Row Yankees in 1923 and from

1926-1928, and he was very good in a limited role in 1927 when he batted .278/.403/.417 as a back-up to "Jumping Joe" Dugan. Though the Yanks went to the World Series in all four of Gazella's seasons with the team, he earned only one plate appearance and made the most of it. In the top of the 10th inning of Game Five, Gazella stepped to the plate after coming in for defensive purposes in the ninth, and was hit by a pitch with Babe Ruth on second and Lou Gehrig on first.

Gazella is one of only two players in history to be hit with a pitch in their only World Series plate appearance.

Vic Raschi (1951): Yankees righty Vic Raschi was known for being a "money" pitcher as evidenced by his career 2.24 ERA in 11 games over six World Series, and from 1950-1952 the "Springfield Rifle" was lights out, going 4-1 with a 0.99 ERA in five starts and one relief appearance. But 1951 provided his oddest stat line.

In Game Three Raschi allowed a second inning RBI single to Willie Mays, but was otherwise in command until the fifth. After striking out Giants pitcher Jim Hearn, Raschi walked Eddie Stanky, who would have been caught stealing second had shortstop Phil Rizzuto not dropped Yogi Berra's throw. But Stanky allegedly kicked the ball from Rizzuto's grasp and not only was he safe but he advanced to third on the error.

Alvin Dark singled Stanky home; Hank Thompson singled Dark to third; Monte Irvin knocked in Dark when Berra dropped third baseman Bobby Brown's throw to the plate; and Whitey Lockman drove Raschi from the box with a three-run homer to right field that gave the Giants a 6-0 lead. Raschi allowed six runs in 4 1/3 innings but only one was earned.

Raschi rebounded and clinched the Series for the Yankees with a Game Six win in which he allowed one run in six innings despite allowing seven hits and walking five. Of course the run was unearned thanks to a Berra passed ball in the fifth, which was clearly Raschi's unlucky inning. He went 1-1 with a 0.87 ERA despite a WHIP of 1.935[1] and is the only pitcher in major league history to allow as many as seven runs in a World Series with only one of them being earned. He's also the only one with a WHIP greater than 1.9 and an ERA less than 1.00.

Joe Christopher (1960): Christopher was a promising talent in the Pirates organization who once hit .366 in the low minors, then batted .317 in AAA from 1958-1960. He debuted with the Pirates in 1959 and was used sparingly, but scored six runs in 15 games without the benefit of a base hit, serving as a valuable pinch runner. "Hurryin' Joe" continued his role as a pinch runner in 1960 and scored 21 runs in 50 games, doing what he could to help Pittsburgh to its first pennant since 1927.

In a Game Two rout that saw the Yankees beat the Pirates, 16-3, Christopher became the second and last player to be hit by a pitch in his only World Series plate appearance when he was plunked by Bob Turley in the bottom of the ninth. Christopher came around to score on consecutive singles by Rocky Nelson and Gino Cimoli, but his run just turned a 16-1 laugher into something a tad less embarrassing.

He scored the Pirates' last run in a 5-2 win in Game Five when he came in to pinch run for Smoky Burgess in the top of the ninth, and ran for Burgess again in the bottom of the seventh of Game Seven, but was erased on a double play. Christopher is the only player to score at least two runs in a World Series and be hit by a pitch in his only plate appearance.

Burt Hooton (1981): From 1971 to 1985 Hooton was one of the best control pitchers in baseball, ranking ninth in walks per nine innings among ERA qualifiers with a 2.71 mark. He enjoyed arguably his best season in 1981 when he pitched to a 2.28 ERA for the

Dodgers who earned a World Series berth against the Yankees for the third time in five years.

Hooton walked a career-low 2.1 batters per nine innings in '81, but his control left him in the postseason where he walked nine hitters in 21 2/3 innings in the NLDS and NLCS. Still, he went 2-0 with 14 2/3 scoreless innings against the Expos in the NLCS and was named MVP of that series. He was almost as good in the World Series, going 1-1 with a 1.59 ERA in two starts, but his pitches were all over the place.

He walked four in six innings in Game Two, then issued five more free passes in Game Six to give him nine more walks in 11 1/3 innings. His 7.15 BB per 9 Innings isn't the worst in World Series history, but it might very well be the most surprising.[2]

Vince Coleman (1987): Coleman immediately established his supremacy as a base thief when he stole 43 bases in 58 Rookie League games in 1982 at the age of 20, then established a new record with 145 steals in 113 games in Single-A in 1983. And that despite missing 31 games with an injury. He stole another 101 in Triple-A in 1984 before making his major league debut in 1985 with the St. Louis Cardinals.

The big leagues intimidated him not at all as he pilfered 110 bases in his rookie season, then followed that up with 107 and 109 in 1986 and '87, respectively. Perhaps as impressive as his totals were his success rates, which averaged 84% in his first three seasons and 81% in 929 attempts in 13 years. So it's no surprise that Coleman went 6 for 6 in stolen base attempts in the 1987 World Series against the Minnesota Twins.

He fell one short of the record held by former Cardinals speedster Lou Brock, who stole seven bases in both the 1967 and '68 Fall Classics. And he tied all-time great Honus Wagner, who swiped six bags in the 1909 Series. But Coleman is only the second man behind

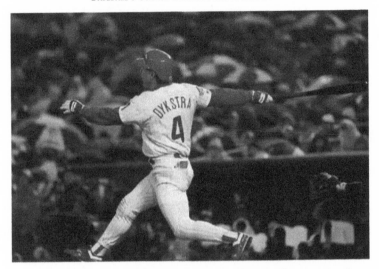

In 1993, Phillies center fielder Lenny Dykstra showed off a power and speed combination never seen before or since in the World Series.

Brock in 1967 to steal as many as six bases in a single Series and not be thrown out.

He also holds the distinction of having the lowest on-base percentage among base thieves with at least four steals in a single World Series at .200, and is tied with Dave Concepcion with those with at least three steals. By contrast Brock posted on-base averages of .452 and .516 in the 1967 and '68 Fall Classics, respectively.

Lenny Dykstra (1993): There are 29 instances in major league history where a player who stole at least 20 bases and hit at least 20 home runs has gone to the World Series. Yet none of them accomplished what Philadelphia Phillies center fielder Lenny Dykstra did in the 1993 Fall Classic against the Toronto Blue Jays.

The 30-year-old Dykstra enjoyed a career year in '93, setting new highs in almost every offensive category, including homers (19) and steals (37). He was very good in the NLCS against the Atlanta

Braves, hitting .280 with two homers, five runs scored, and an OPS of .960. But he really came alive in the World Series, batting .348 with four circuit clouts, nine runs, eight RBIs, and four steals, and posted a 1.413 OPS that stands third all-time among batters with at least 30 plate appearances.

Only Barry Bonds (1.994 in 2002) and Babe Ruth (1.448 in 1926) were better, but Dykstra accomplished a feat that no other player has even come close to—he belted four homers and stole four bases in the same World Series. Davey Lopes hit three homers and stole two bags for the '78 Dodgers; Fred Clarke had two homers and three steals for the '09 Tigers, as did Kirk Gibson for the '84 Tigers, and Chase Utley for the 2008 Phillies. But Dykstra is the only member of the 4/4 club in Fall Classic history.

Pat Burrell (2010): Burrell never led the league in strikeouts but it wasn't for a lack of effort. The slugger whiffed 1,564 times in 1,640 career games over 12 years, mostly with the Phillies, but also belted 292 home runs for an average of 29 per 162 games. In his prime from 2005-2008 Burrell averaged 31 long balls a year and slugged .504. He landed in Tampa Bay via free agency in 2009 before signing with the San Francisco Giants on May 29, 2010.

The 33-year-old was fantastic with San Francisco, slugging .509 with 18 homers and 51 RBIs in 96 games and helped the Giants advance to the World Series against the Texas Rangers. Despite a career strikeout percentage of almost 24%, no one expected Burrell to fan in almost every at-bat, but that's almost what he did, striking out 11 times in 13 at-bats. That's not a record for most strikeouts in a World Series but every other batter who fanned at least 10 times in a single Fall Classic had at least 21 at bats.

He Ain't Heavy...He's a Boyer

Although they were born almost six years apart, Ken and Clete Boyer made their major league debuts in 1955; 24-year-old Ken on April 12 with the St. Louis Cardinals and 18-year-old Clete with the Kansas City A's. Their careers took divergent paths as Ken quickly established himself as one of the best third baseman of the postwar era, while Clete struggled to earn a roster spot until 1960 when he became the Yankees' starting third baseman.

By then Ken was already an established star, having been named to three National League All-Star teams and copping three Gold Glove awards from 1955-1960, during which he batted .293 and averaged 24 home runs and 84 RBIs a season. He earned four more All-Star berths and two more Gold Gloves from 1961-1964, and enjoyed one of his best seasons in '64 when he was named the NL's Most Valuable Player thanks in part to a league-leading 119 RBIs.

Clete wasn't the hitter his older brother was—from 1960-1964 he hit .242 and averaged 13 homers and 55 RBIs per season—but he was one of the best third basemen in the game and would go down as "one of the best glove men ever" at the hot corner.[1] And Bill James gave him a rating of A+ in his book *Win Shares*, the only postwar era third baseman to receive a mark that high.[2]

The 1964 World Series marked the fifth time the Cardinals and Yankees would meet in October—St. Louis won in 1926 and '42; the

The 1964 Fall Classic pitted Ken (left) and Clete Boyer against each other. They'd set a record in Game Seven that still stands.

Yanks in 1928 and '43—but it almost didn't happen. The Cardinals didn't win the pennant until the last day of the season when they beat the Mets, 11-5, and the Phillies routed the Reds, 10-0. The Yankees clinched a bit sooner, but still finished only a game ahead of the Chicago White Sox. With their Series history tied at two wins apiece, 1964 would prove to be the rubber match.

St. Louis took Game One, 9-5, at Busch Stadium, but New York knotted the Series with an 8-3 win in Game Two. The Series shifted to Yankee Stadium and wins were traded again with the Yanks taking Game Three, 2-1, and the Cards taking Game Four, 4-3 on the strength of a Ken Boyer sixth inning grand slam. St. Louis won Game Five in thrilling fashion when Tim McCarver belted a three-run homer in the 10th inning to lead his club to a 5-2 win. New York tied the Series again at three games apiece thanks to homers by

Mickey Mantle, Roger Maris, and Joe Pepitone in Game Six, and the teams met at Busch Stadium for a seventh game to decide the whole enchilada.

Twenty-two-year-old rookie right hander Mel Stottlemyre took the hill for the Yankees and faced 28-year-old veteran Bob Gibson, who was starting to build one of the best postseason resumes in baseball history. Neither team scored through the first three innings, and Gibson put up another goose egg in the top of the fourth. The Cards reached Stottlemyre for three runs in the bottom of the fourth thanks in part to Ken Boyer who singled and scored on a McCarver groundout.

Gibson set New York down again in the fifth before his teammates roughed up new Yankees hurler Al Downing for three more runs in the bottom of the frame. Again, Boyer played a role with a double and a run scored. The Bronx Bombers refused to quit, though, and halved the score at 6-3 when Mantle launched a three-run bomb in the top of the sixth.

Neither team plated a runner in the bottom of the sixth or top of the seventh, but Ken struck again when he homered to left in the bottom of the seventh to give the Cards a 7-3 lead. Then the game got interesting again when Clete made history with a homer of his own in the top of the ninth that pulled the Yanks to within 7-4. It was the first and only time brothers have homered in the same World Series game. Phil Linz touched Gibson for another solo shot, but Gibson got Bobby Richardson to pop out for the final out of the game and Series.

Ken made a little history of his own when he became the first Cardinal to homer more than once in the same World Series. Neither Boyer would play in another World Series.

The Mickey Lolich Miracle

Say the name Mickey Lolich and most baseball fans will immediately think of the 1968 World Series and the portly Tigers lefty who almost single-handedly beat the St. Louis Cardinals in seven games. Lolich won Games Two, Five, and Seven, beating Bob Gibson to send the championship back to Detroit for the first time since 1945. Gibson was 7-1 in World Series play when Lolich defeated him, 4-1, on October 10, 1968 in what would prove to be the Cardinal legend's final World Series start.

But what some might not realize is that the Portland, Oregon native was one of the worst hitters in major league history. Lolich never topped the Mendoza line in his 16-year career and recorded an anemic .110 batting average with no home runs in 1,107 plate appearances. He batted a career-high .197 in 1967 and that was as good as it got. He also hit .056 in 1963, .058 in 1965, .067 in 1972, and .088 in 1969. In fact, he was so bad at the plate that of his 90 career hits only seven went for extra bases—five doubles and two triples—and three of those came in 1968.

Lolich finished second on the club with 17 wins, but his 3.19 ERA was actually subpar in a league where the average ERA was 2.98. Among Tigers hurlers who made starts on the year, Lolich ranked behind McLain, Earl Wilson, Pat Dobson, and John Hiller in earned run average. In fact, a rough stretch in July during which he went 3-4 with a 7.07 ERA from July 5 to July 28 knocked him from the rotation until August 22.

He was 7-7 with a 3.61 ERA on July 28, but turned things around and won his next four decisions out of the bullpen, fashioning a scoreless streak that lasted 15 1/3 innings and reduced his ERA to 3.40. After two consecutive impressive relief outings in which he allowed only five hits in 10 2/3 innings, Lolich was reinstated to the rotation and he rewarded skipper Mayo Smith by going 6-2 with a 2.61 ERA in his last nine starts, which included three of his four shutouts on the year.

Fast forward to Game Two of the '68 Series with the Cardinals holding a one game lead after Gibson defeated 31-game winner Denny McLain in Game One in St. Louis. Cards Manager Red Schoendienst tabbed 25-year-old 19-game winner Nelson Briles to take the hill against Lolich in the second tilt. Briles was in his first year as a starter after spending most of his time in the bullpen from 1965-1967. Over those three seasons, he recorded 21 wins and 16 saves, posted a very good 2.96 ERA, and led the National League in winning percentage at .737 in 1967.

Lolich was almost scratched from his start in favor of Joe Sparma when Smith learned from the team doctor that his southpaw had an infected boil near his groin that required medication that could have affected Lolich's stamina. But Smith sent him out there and hoped for the best. And the best is what he got.

Briles set the Tigers down in order in the first. Lolich worked out of a two-on, one-out jam to keep the game scoreless after one thanks in part to a great catch by Al Kaline, who corralled Orlando Cepeda's long foul in front of the bullpen door in right field for the second out of the inning. The Tigers quickly broke the deadlock when Detroit's leading home run hitter, Willie Horton, blasted a Briles offering over the 386-foot mark in left field to "break the ice."[1]

Tigers lefty Mickey Lolich defeated the Cardinals three times in the 1968 World Series, but it was an at-bat in Game Two that took everyone by surprise, including Lolich himself.

"We've been in a slump since the last Baltimore series," said pinch hitter extraordinaire Gates Brown. "I enjoy days like this when all I have to do is sit back and watch the guys go around the bases."[2] Lolich had an easier time with the Cardinals in the second, setting them down in order, then he helped himself out in the top of the third when the absurd happened—he deposited a homer into the left field seats and became the first player in big league history to homer in a World Series despite never hitting one at any other point in his career.[3]

Lolich was so stunned he missed first base and had to go back and touch it. "I swung and saw it start, but I didn't know where it was going," he said after the game. "I was watching the leftfielder, and then I heard the crowd yell. So when I got to first I didn't tag the base. I stepped right over it."[4]

On the mound, Lolich's only misstep came in the sixth inning when he tried to make a play on a Curt Flood grounder between the mound and third base, but slipped and couldn't make a throw. "Had Lolich let the ball alone, [Don] Wert could have handled it," wrote Clif Keane. "But Mickey was anxious, grabbed the ball, and as he started to turn to throw to first, lost his balance."[5] That put runners on first and third with one out—Lou Brock walked and stole second before Julian Javier struck out.

Orlando Cepeda dumped a single behind second base to plate Brock and give the Cardinals their first run of the game. But Lolich and the Tigers held a 5-1 lead thanks to a Norm Cash solo homer in the top of the sixth and a Dick McAuliffe two-run single. Lolich cruised from there and Detroit won easily by a score of 8-1. He added a single in the eighth, then walked with the bases loaded in the ninth and drove in his second run of the game. Had he knocked in a third run, he would have equaled his total for the entire season.

Lolich defeated Briles again in Game Five, then bested Gibson in Game Seven to lead the Tigers to their third World Series title in franchise history.

Protest Flags, Vietnam,
and the 1969 Mets

By the time 1969 rolled around there were more than 500,000 U.S. military personnel in Vietnam fighting a war that would take the lives of more than 58,000 American soldiers and wound more than 150,000. Active American combat units were first employed in March 1965, and anti-war protestors had finally had enough and planned a massive rally in cities all over the country.

The Vietnam Moratorium Committee was formed by Sam Brown, a staff aide to Minnesota Senator Eugene McCarthy; David Mixner, a former McCarthy staffer who joined a committee helmed by South Dakota Senator George McGovern designed to reform the Democratic party; and draft resistor David Hawk.[1] The Vietnam Moratorium Committee was prepared to stage a protest on October 15, 1969 if there was "no firm commitment to American withdrawal [from Vietnam] or a negotiated settlement."[2]

The Committee's goal was to recruit college students, community organizations, churches, professional groups, labor unions, civil rights groups, politicians, and "even high school students" for the October rally.[3] On July 1 it was reported that at least 100 campuses across the United States had pledged their support.[4]

On September 28 the New York Times reported that activities on October 15 would include classroom boycotts, mass rallies, candlelight parades, memorial services in churches, and "ceremonies for reading the rolls of those killed in Vietnam."[5] President Richard Nixon was unmoved. "Under no circumstances will I be affected whatever by it," Nixon announced.[6]

"Massive antiwar demonstrations were expected throughout the country today despite President Nixon's statement that the agitation was undercutting his efforts for an honorable peace," wrote Homer Bigart on October 15.[7] Americans who supported the Vietnam Moratorium Committee were instructed to lower their American flags to half-staff. Opposition to the movement insisted on keeping their flags at full-staff and planned on driving with their headlights on during daylight hours in support of the president.[8]

New York Mayor John Lindsay chose to participate in the anti-war rallies despite resistance from veterans, police, and fire fighters, who refused to fly their flags at half-staff. "This moratorium is a peaceful thing," Lindsay insisted, "prayerful in manner, to protest this war...It is a peaceful, prayerful alternative to violent confrontation."[9]

Lindsay had ordered all public buildings to fly their flags at half-staff, including Shea Stadium where the Mets were to host the Baltimore Orioles in Game Four of the World Series. There was to be a pregame flag ceremony that featured a military color guard, a band, and 225 wounded Vietnam War veterans, but shortly before the ceremony they "announced they would not participate unless the flag was flown full-staff."[10]

The National Anthem was to be performed by the United States Merchant Marine Academy Band of Kings Point, Long Island, but when they learned the flag would be flown at half-staff they failed to appear on the field.[11] Major League Commissioner Bowie Kuhn intervened and ordered the flag at Shea to fly full-staff.

"In accordance with interested parties, including involved military personnel and the Mayor of New York" Kuhn announced, "I have decided to fly the Shea Stadium flags at full staff today. The Mayor requested that I take whatever step would promote the greatest amount of respect and quiet in the stadium and I have concluded that this step would comply with his request."[12]

Shirley Povich wrote that Kuhn had no doubt "heard from his bosses, the club owners, who asked if he was some kind of a nut or something about this war moratorium nonsense, and to remember that baseball was the Great American Game, and that they had a say in this, and that the flag would go all the way up the pole..."[13]

Twenty-four-year-old Mets ace and first time Cy Young Award winner Tom Seaver pitched one of the most masterful games in World Series history when he held Baltimore to only one run in 10 innings in Game Four to lead the Mets to a 2-1 victory that staked New York to a three-games-to-one lead in a Series they'd win the next day. But Seaver wasn't happy with the off-the-field controversy and he vented after the game.

The *Washington Post* reported that moratorium supporters were outside of Shea Stadium handing out leaflets that quoted Seaver as saying that the United States should get out of Vietnam. Seaver did, in fact, state that he thought the U.S. should get out of Vietnam and called our involvement "perfectly ridiculous" and "absurd," and claimed that he wanted to take out an ad in the *New York Times* that read: "If the Mets can win the World Series, then we can get out of Vietnam."[14]

He admitted to what he said, but was upset that moratorium organizers used his picture and quotes without permission. "I'm a ballplayer, not a politician," he told reporters. "But I'm an American citizen, and I have my feelings. They shouldn't be blown out of proportion."[15]

The Mets won Game Five and their first World Series title behind Jerry Koosman and Donn Clendenon. Ironically, the U.S. withdrew most of its troops from Vietnam in 1973, the next time the Mets won the National League pennant. Alas, although they pushed the Oakland A's to seven games, the Mets fared no better in the World Series than the United States did in the Vietnam War.

The Ultimate Fall Classic: Game Six

October 21, 1975—Cincinnati Reds at Boston Red Sox: The 1975 World Series between the Cincinnati Reds and Boston Red Sox is arguably the greatest Fall Classic ever played, and Game Six had a lot to do with that. After Boston cult hero and whirling dervish Luis Tiant blanked the "Big Red Machine" in Game One for a 6-0 victory, the Series became a back-and-forth affair in which Games Two through Four were decided by one run.

The Reds plated two in the top of the ninth of Game Two to win, 3-2; Boston scored two in the top of the ninth of Game Three to force extra innings, only to lose, 6-5 in 10 innings; then Tiant came back and tossed a gutsy Game Four in which he threw 163 pitches in a complete-game, 5-4 win. Game Five went to the Reds, 6-2, behind staff ace Don Gullett.

Heading into Game Six at Fenway Park, Cincinnati needed only one win to cop its first World Series title since 1940. The Red Sox needed to win the next two to grab their first championship since 1918.

Cincinnati had dominated the regular season, going 108-54 and finishing 20 games ahead of second-place Los Angeles, before sweeping the Pittsburgh Pirates in convincing fashion to earn its third pennant of the decade. They boasted baseball's best offense, plating 5.19 runs per game, the third lowest ERA at 3.37, and the second most efficient defense. The Reds' roster included the NL MVP in Joe Morgan and four men who would eventually be inducted into the Hall of Fame—Johnny Bench, Morgan, Tony Perez and manager Sparky Anderson—and a fifth, Pete Rose, who would have been if not for his gambling addiction.

The Red Sox went 95-65, edged the Baltimore Orioles by four and a half games, then swept the three-time defending AL champion Oakland A's in the ALCS. They led the league in runs per game at 4.97, but their pitching staff ranked ninth in the league with a subpar 3.98 ERA, and they were only a hair above average on defense. Boston boasted the league MVP and Rookie of the Year in Fred Lynn and three future Hall of Famers in Carl Yastrzemski, Carlton Fisk, and rookie Jim Rice. Unfortunately, Rice was knocked out of action when his hand was broken by a Vern Ruhle pitch on September 21 and wasn't available to the Red Sox in the postseason.

On the other hand, Rice's injury forced Yastrzemski from first base and back to his old familiar left field spot, where he dominated the A's with diving stabs, leaping catches at the Green Monster and laser throws that cut down Oakland runners on the base paths or kept them from advancing. Yaz also made a play on a Reggie Jackson hit that was so impressive the slugger later waxed, "Only two people could have made that play: Carl Yastrzemski and God."[1]

The World Series had been dogged by wet weather and things got especially bad between Games Five and Six, forcing the teams to wait out a rain storm that soaked the Fens and caused the sixth tilt to be postponed three times before the Series resumed on October 21.

Once Game Six finally began, Tiant dispatched the Reds on 15 pitches, retiring Rose, Morgan and Bench around a one-out walk to Ken Griffey. Reds starter Gary Nolan was not so successful, surrendering two-out singles to Yaz and Fisk and a three-run homer to Lynn to give the Red Sox an early 3-0 lead.

Tiant and Nolan traded goose eggs in the second, but Anderson, known as "Captain Hook" because of his propensity to remove pitchers at the first sign of trouble, replaced Nolan with a pinch hitter in the top of the third after the righty had faced only nine batters.

Tiant was efficient in the third, using only eight pitches to set down Cesar Geronimo, pinch hitter Darrel Chaney and Ken Griffey, wrapped around a Pete Rose two-out single. With three lefties coming up in succession in the bottom of the third, Anderson turned to southpaw Fred Norman, who'd spent most of the season in the rotation and fashioned a 12-4 record with a 3.73 ERA in 34 appearances. Norman retired Cecil Cooper on a pop up, then surrendered a double to Denny Doyle before coaxing Yaz to pop to Morgan. An intentional walk to right-handed hitting Carlton Fisk put men on first and second, then an unintentional walk to Lynn loaded the bases and ended Norman's night. Jack Billingham was summoned and fanned Rico Petrocelli to end the threat.

Tiant began the fourth by retiring Morgan and Bench, but Perez singled to right, then went to third on a throwing error by short-stop Rick Burleson, who threw past Doyle on a force attempt on a George Foster ground ball. Tiant squelched the rally by getting Concepcion to pop out to Cooper at first. Billingham also had to snuff out a scoring threat in his half of the fourth when Dwight Evans led off with a ground-rule double to right and Burleson walked to put runners at first and second with nobody out. Tiant sacrificed the runners to second and third, but Cooper and Doyle both grounded out to end the inning with the Red Sox still up 3-0.

The portly, herky-jerky Cuban's luck finally ran out in the fifth and one play almost lost the Sox their star center fielder. Geronimo flied out to Evans to begin the inning, bringing up controversial pinch hitter Ed Armbrister, who came in for Billingham. It was a bunt by Armbrister in the bottom of the 10th inning of Game Three that resulted in one of the most debated plays in World Series history and made home plate umpire Larry Barnett a household name. With Geronimo on first, Armbrister laid down a sacrifice bunt that Fisk quickly recovered and fired to second for the force. Fisk's throw soared over second base and into center field, and the runners advanced to second and third with no outs and the winning run only 90 feet from pay dirt.

Fisk and Armbrister collided on the play and it appeared as if Armbrister purposely stopped in front of the Boston backstop on his way to first, or was confused about how to proceed out of the batter's box and on to first base. Either way, a brief collision ensued and the Reds benefited greatly from it. Pudge was livid and insisted Barnett call interference on the play. Darrell Johnson ran out to argue but got nowhere. Fisk would later be second-guessed as on-lookers wondered why he didn't just tag Armbrister and take the easy out. Three batters later, Morgan singled in the winning run and the Reds went up two games to one.

This time, though, there was no controversy; Armbrister walked on five pitches, went to third on a single by Rose, and both came home on a Griffey triple to deep center field that Lynn appeared to have momentarily before crashing hard into the outfield wall and collapsing in a heap. The former USC Trojan football player toughed it out, though, and remained in the game.

After Morgan popped to third for the second out, Bench singled off the Green Monster to tie the score at 3-3. Then Tiant fanned Perez to end the inning. Thirty-four-year-old Clay Carroll brought his 2.62 ERA into the game in the bottom of the fifth and gave up a lead-off single to Yastrzemski before retiring Fisk, Lynn and Petrocelli in order. "El Tiante" walked a tightrope again in the sixth, surrendering two-out singles to Geronimo and pinch hitter Terry Crowley, but retired Rose on a pop up to Burleson to escape the jam.

Nine-game winner Pedro Borbon became Cincinnati's fifth pitcher of the game when he took the mound in the bottom of the sixth, and except for a one-out walk to Burleson, he was perfect, setting down Evans, Tiant, and Cooper. Tiant finally relinquished the lead in the top of the seventh on another extra-base hit, this time off the bat of Foster who doubled with two outs and two on to plate Griffey and Morgan and give the Reds a 5-3 lead.

Borbon needed only eight pitches to get through the seventh, then Cincinnati increased its lead to 6-3 when Geronimo wrapped a homer around the right field foul pole. Tiant was finally removed in favor of Roger Moret and left the field to a standing ovation and chants of "Loo-ee, Loo-ee," a serenade Red Sox fans used to cheer on their favorite hurler.

Moret retired the side with relative ease, setting up one of the most exciting and memorable half-innings in World Series history. Borbon entered his third inning of work by allowing a single to Lynn and a free pass to Petrocelli, which brought the tying run to the plate in the form of Dewey Evans. Anderson yanked Borbon in favor of closer Rawley Eastwick, a 24-year-old rookie with a 2.60 regular-season ERA and a league-best 22 saves. Evans worked the count full before fanning for the first out, then Burleson lined out to left and it looked like the Reds would escape with their three-run lead intact.

But Johnson had an ace in the hole—Bernie Carbo, a left-handed slugger with a .483 slugging percentage who was drafted by Cincinnati in 1965 and finished second in NL Rookie of the Year voting in 1970. Carbo's temper and half-hearted approach to the game earned him two less-than-flattering nicknames in the minors—"The Idiot" and "The Clown." Anderson took Carbo under his wing, though, and the youngster blossomed in 1969 with Double-A Indianapolis, batting .359 with 21 homers and 76 RBIs in 111 games. Still, Carbo would never become anything more than a platoon player during his 12 seasons in the majors.

When Bernie stepped to the plate in the eighth inning of Game Six, he'd already made his mark on the Series with a pinch hit home run in the seventh inning of Game Three off Carroll. Now the man Bill Lee once described as "pure oxygen looking for a flame" had a chance to put his team back into the game.

Sparky went against the book and left the right-handed throwing Eastwick in to face Carbo. It wasn't as risky a move as one might think, considering Eastwick was actually better against lefties than righties that season, and he made Carbo look absolutely foolish on a 2-2 pitch that Carbo barely fouled off with a swing that he admitted later was the single worst swing in the history of baseball.

But the foul tip gave him life and he made the most of it. Eastwick's next offering caught too much of the plate and Carbo lofted it deep into the night toward the center field stands where it finally nestled for a game-tying three-run homer. With his second pinch homer Carbo tied a record set by Chuck Essegian, who turned the same trick for the Dodgers in 1959.

Johnson shuffled his lineup by bringing closer Dick Drago into the game, sending Carbo out to left and bringing Yaz in to play first. Drago's task was not easy. When he entered the game he was greeted by the heart of the Reds' lineup, composed of three future Hall of Famers—Morgan, Bench, and Perez. But the mustachioed bullpen ace made it look easy, getting two pop ups and a ground out.

Eastwick came out for the bottom of the ninth and ran into immediate trouble, walking Doyle and surrendering a single to Yaz to put runners at first and third with no outs. Anderson pulled Eastwick and called on Will McEnaney, who had the unenviable task of facing Fisk, Lynn and Petrocelli, Boston's 4-5-6 hitters. Anderson ordered an intentional walk of Fisk to load the bases and set up a force at any base.

Lynn lofted one to shallow left, right down the line. Don Zimmer, coaching at third, told Doyle to tag up, but when he saw how shallow Lynn's fly was, he held up his hands and shouted "No! No! No!" Doyle explained later that he heard Zimmer yelling "Go! Go! Go!" So he did, and was gunned down by Foster at the plate. Suddenly the Sox had two outs and runners at first and second. McEnaney retired Petrocelli on a grounder to Rose and the game went into extra frames.

It was still Tuesday, October 21 but before long it would roll into the early morning hours of Wednesday, October 22. Drago came out for the 10th and surrendered a one-out single to Concepcion, who then promptly stole second, but settled down to strike out Geronimo and retire pinch hitter Dan Driessen on a short fly ball to Carbo that he almost botched, probably because he was wasted.

"I played every game high," Carbo admitted years later. "I was addicted to anything you could possibly be addicted to." Before Game Six, Carbo speculated that he "probably smoked two joints, drank about three or four beers...took some amphetamines, took a pain pill, drank a cup of coffee, chewed some tobacco and had a cigarette" before his eighth inning at-bat.[2]

In the bottom of the 10th, Anderson called his eighth pitcher into the game, 11-game winner Pat Darcy, who won only 14 games in a career that lasted three years. The skipper's only other options were Clay Kirby and staff ace Don Gullett, who was penciled in as Cincinnati's Game Seven starter.

Darcy and Drago battled to a draw for the next inning and a half, the only blemish to either's pitching line a pitch from the latter that plunked Rose to lead off the top of the 11th. It could have been much worse for Drago and the Red Sox but for a spectacular circus catch and throw by Dwight Evans that Anderson later insisted was the greatest catch he'd ever seen. With Rose on first, Griffey laid down a bunt designed to move "Charlie Hustle" to second, but Fisk refused to concede and gunned Rose down for the force. It looked like the failed sacrifice attempt would be lost in time when Morgan jumped all over a Drago offering and lined it toward the right field seats for what appeared to be a go-ahead two-run homer. But Evans raced to the wall, tracking the ball over his right shoulder and moving toward the right field line.

Because of the path the future eight-time Gold Glover took, he had to leap and thrust out his left hand at the last moment, essentially reaching back behind his head to make the catch, made all the more difficult when Evans briefly lost sight of the ball. Evans then bounced off the waist high fence, turned and fired the ball to Yastrzemski, who ranged far off the bag and past the coach's box to retrieve the throw, then tossed to an alert Burleson, who raced over to cover the first base bag and doubled off Griffey.

The game went into the 12th and Johnson turned to staff ace Rick Wise, a supremely talented athlete who won a team-leading 19 games during the regular season and once belted two home runs in a game in which he also tossed a no-hitter. Wise won Game Three of the ALCS before being trounced by Cincinnati in Game Three of the World Series.

Since Geronimo's homer in the eighth, only two Reds had gotten to first base, Concepcion in the 10th and Rose in the 11th, but they put two of their first three hitters on in the top of the 12th. Perez and Foster rapped consecutive singles to put men at first and second with one out. Concepcion flied to Evans in right but not deep enough to advance the runners, then Wise fanned Geronimo to end the threat.

The clock stood at approximately 12:30 AM when Carlton Fisk stepped into the box to take the first hacks of Boston's half of the 12th. Fisk, a New England native, was born in Vermont and grew up in New Hampshire, so he was well aware of the Red Sox's history of late-Series failures in Fall Classic play. But the husky catcher went to the plate with a plan, telling Lynn that he was going to bang a shot off the Green Monster, and that it was up to the rookie center fielder to drive him in.

Fisk took Darcy's first offering for a ball. Darcy came back with a pitch down and in, and Fisk went down and got it, golfing it high into the early morning sky and toward the left field foul pole. Fisk knew how the wind typically reacted at Fenway Park and was afraid his fly ball would be pushed foul, so he instinctively began hopping up the first base line, waving his arms in a way that he hoped would somehow keep the ball fair.

The ball struck the wire mesh of the foul pole high above the playing field for a game-winning, walk-off homer that sent the World Series to a seventh game. Like the Kennedy assassination, the moon walk, the eruption of Washington's Mt. St. Helens, most remember where they were when Fisk's drive decided Game Six, 7-6. All of New England was in hysterics. Fans mobbed the field inside Fenway, and citizens mobbed the streets outside. Church bells rang in Charlestown, New Hampshire where Fisk grew up.

Sticking to the script, the Reds and Red Sox battled to a 3-3 tie through eight innings of Game Seven, taking the game into the final frame all knotted up in a winner-take-all battle. Gullett, the ace Los Angeles Times writer Jim Murray wanted to see in Game Six, lasted only four innings and allowed all three Boston runs. Lee, the eccentric lefty who was skipped over in Game Six in favor of Tiant, went 6 1/3 innings and allowed all three Cincinnati runs. Finally, in the top of the ninth, Morgan drove in Griffey with a looping liner to center that dropped just in front of Lynn to give the Reds a 4-3 lead. When Yaz lofted an easy fly to Geronimo with two outs in the bottom of the ninth, the Reds had their first championship in 35 years.

The 1975 Fall Classic featured five games that were decided by one run, two of which went into extra innings, and four of which were decided in the winning team's final at-bat, making it arguably the greatest World Series ever played.

Jim Palmer Walks Like a Man

Baltimore Orioles legend and Hall of Famer Jim Palmer was one of the best hurlers in postseason history and is among only five starting pitchers to have won at least eight games while posting an ERA of 2.61 or better. But, like Mickey Lolich, he was a poor hitter. From 1965-1972, Palmer batted .174 with three home runs and 207 strikeouts in 489 at-bats. Fortunately the American League adopted the designated hitter rule in 1973 and spared us from having to watch Palmer bat again until the 1979 World Series when he went 0 for 4 with three whiffs.

In his seven years as a "hitter" Palmer drew only 16 walks, never earning more than three free passes in any one season. In 1971 the right hander went 20-9 with a 2.68 ERA and somehow managed to receive not a single Cy Young Award vote. He batted .196 and found enough holes in opposing defenses to drive in a career-high nine runs. He also walked three times in 116 plate appearances.

Palmer's Orioles faced the Pittsburgh Pirates in the '71 Fall Classic in a fantastic match-up of teams that won 101 and 97 games, respectively, and featured six Hall of Famers, split evenly between the two combatants. Southpaw Dave McNally led the O's to a 5-3 win in Game One and Palmer got the ball for Game Two. Palmer struggled with his control and walked eight in eight innings of work, but a Richie Hebner three-run homer in the eighth was the only blemish on his ledger as Baltimore cruised to a convincing 11-3 victory.

But it's what Palmer accomplished at the plate that made his outing truly stand out. With the Orioles sporting a 1-0 lead over Bob Johnson going into the fourth, Baltimore mounted a rally. Frank Robinson singled with one out, Elrod Hendricks was hit with a pitch, and Brooks Robinson walked to load the bases. Davey Johnson knocked in Robinson and Hendricks with a single to stake the Orioles to a 3-0 lead and Johnson's day was over.

Twenty-one-year-old rookie Bruce Kison entered the game and promptly walked Mark Belanger to reload the bases. That brought up Palmer and the impossible happened—Kison walked him on four pitches to make the score 4-0. Bob Moose took over mound duties and was the beneficiary of Don Buford's fly out to Willie Stargell in left, who gunned down Johnson at the plate for an inning-ending double play.

Palmer sandwiched two strikeouts and a line out around a Stargell free pass in the top of the fifth, then Baltimore's batters went back to work in the bottom of the frame. Merv Rettenmund and Boog Powell greeted Moose with consecutive singles, and the former advanced to third on a deep fly to right by Frank Robinson. Hendricks singled in Rettenmund and Powell, and went all the way to third on an error by center fielder Al Oliver.

Brooks Robinson singled in Hendricks and the rout was on. Johnson singled and forced Pirates skipper Danny Murtaugh to go to his bullpen once again, this time calling on 35-year-old veteran Bob Veale, who posted a career-worst 6.99 ERA in 37 regular season games, and led the National League in walks four times in a five-year span from 1964-1968. So it's no surprise that he followed Kison's script and walked Belanger to load the bases. Then he did the unthinkable and walked Palmer again to send yet another Orioles runner across the plate.

Palmer finished his hitting "prowess" with a groundout to first baseman Bob Robertson in the sixth, then polished off the Pirates in the seventh before surrendering Hebner's homer in the eighth and passing the torch to Dick Hall, who finished off the Pirates in the ninth to cap off an 11-3 Orioles win.

The Pirates came back from a two-games-to-one deficit to defeat the Orioles in seven games, but Palmer set a record that still stands, becoming the only hitter in World Series history to drive in two runs on two walks but no hits.[1]

Bruce Kison Comes to Earth

The 1979 Pittsburgh Pirates capped off a great decade with another World Series win over the Baltimore Orioles, repeating their 1971 victory over the same Orioles, albeit with a different squad. From 1970-1979 Pittsburgh won six division titles, two pennants, and two World Series titles, and pitcher Bruce Kison played a major role in most of it. Kison was a 21-year-old rookie in 1971 but he developed a reputation as a "money" pitcher when he allowed only three hits in 11 postseason innings, and held the powerful Orioles to one hit in 6 1/3 innings of relief in the '71 Fall Classic.

But his postseason career got off to a rocky start when he walked the first two batters he faced, including opposing pitcher Jim Palmer with the bases loaded. The run was charged to Bob Johnson, though, so Kison's record remained unblemished. He also hit three batters, including Frank Robinson.

He continued his scoreless streak in 1972 with another 2 1/3 brilliant innings against the Cincinnati Reds in the NLCS, then ran his postseason record to a perfect 4-0 with a win over the Los Angeles Dodgers in the 1974 NLCS. It wasn't until the seventh inning of Game Three of the 1975 NLCS against the Reds that Kison finally allowed a run, but he tacked on another scoreless inning after that to drop his suddenly existent ERA to 0.41 in seven post-season appearances.

Pirates pitcher Bruce Kison (left) was mostly fantastic in his postseason career, but suffered a record-setting hiccup in the 1979 World Series.

Kison battled blister problems in 1979, but went 13-7 and led the rotation with a 3.19 ERA. He heated up late in the season and went 5-0 with a 1.74 ERA in his last seven starts, but manager Chuck Tanner didn't need him in the NLCS against the Reds, so Kison was well-rested going into Game One of the World Series. Perhaps too well rested, especially after the game was postponed due to rain. After Orioles lefty Mike Flanagan stranded Dave Parker on second in the top of the first, Kison completely melted down in the bottom half.

Al Bumbry led off the stanza with a single, went to second on a walk to Mark Belanger, and both advanced 90 feet when Kison dropped Ken Singleton's one-hopper to the mound that should have resulted in a double play, but went for only one out. Eddie Murray walked to load the bases, but John Lowenstein grounded to second baseman Phil Garner and the Pirates should have been out of the inning but for Garner's poor throw.

"The ball was soaking wet when it got to me and felt like a bar of soap," Garner insisted after the game."When I went to throw it, it went out of my hand like soap."[1] Garner chucked the ball into left field and two runs scored to give the O's a 2-0 lead. Kison unloaded a wild pitch that plated Murray, surrendered a two-run homer to Doug DeCinces, and saw his day end mercifully after Billy Smith singled. Jim Rooker, Enrique Romo, Don Robinson, and Grant Jackson held the Orioles scoreless for the rest of the game, but Flanagan escaped with a well-earned 5-4 win.

Kison faced seven batters, retired only one of them, and finished the Series with an ERA of 108.00, the highest ERA ever recorded by a pitcher in a single World Series among those who recorded at least one out. He returned to form in 1982 when he went 1-0 with a 1.93 ERA in two starts for the California Angels in the ALCS and finished his postseason career with a 5-1 mark and a stellar 1.98 ERA.

Fortunately for Kison, his record would stand for only a year. In 1980 Philadelphia Phillies pitcher Larry Christenson suffered the same fate, except he didn't have Kison's impressive postseason resume to fall back on. Prior to his Game Four start in the 1980 World Series against the Kansas City Royals, Christenson had only pitched in the NLCS, twice against the Dodgers in 1977 and 1978, and once against the Houston Astros in 1980, and his postseason ERA was 7.54 through 14 1/3 innings.

The Phillies held a two-games-to-one lead going into Game Four at Royals Stadium and were counting on Christenson to put the Phillies one win away from their first championship in franchise history, a tall order for a pitcher who missed most of the season after having bone chips removed from his elbow in late May. The Washington native made eight starts after the surgery and was very good, going 2-1 with a 2.81 ERA in 48 innings, and was excellent in his only start against Houston in the NLCS, but was touched for three earned runs in only two-thirds of an inning in his Game Five relief appearance.

After Dennis Leonard dispatched the Phillies in the top of the first, Willie Wilson led off the bottom of the inning with a single that broke a 1 for 13 slump, then scampered to third when Christenson threw a pickoff attempt past first for a two-base error. Frank White flied to short right field before the flood gates opened; George Brett tripled to score Wilson, then came home on Willie Aiken's two-run bomb, his third homer of the Series.

Hal McRae and Amos Otis slapped consecutive doubles to push the Royals' lead to 4-0 and that ended Christenson's brief and disastrous outing. Aikens homered again off Dickie Noles, but Philadelphia's bullpen did an outstanding job keeping the Phillies in a game they'd eventually lose, 5-3. They recovered to win Games Five and Six to cop their first ever championship, but Christenson will live in infamy as the last pitcher to post an ERA of 108.00 in a single World Series.

Lonnie Smith: Braves' Hero

by Walter Friedman

Lonnie Smith's failure to score in the 8th inning of Game Seven of the 1991 World Series is commonly considered one of the most costly October blunders of all time. With the score 0-0, Smith led off the inning with a single, and when Terry Pendleton followed with a double in the gap, Smith paused before reaching second and was only able to advance to third. The Braves failed to score in the inning, and Jack Morris tacked on two more scoreless innings before the Twins pushed across the series-winning run in the bottom of the 10th.

Smith, who had a solid career that includes a lifetime batting average of .288 and an OBA of .371, is now largely remembered for the misplay, just as Bill Buckner's blunder in Game Six of the 1986 World Series has obscured his great career that included over 2700 hits and 1200 RBI. And just as there is a lot of injustice in Buckner being blamed for the loss—the Mets had already tied the game—Lonnie Smith should not be considered a goat given the considerable failures of his teammates, plus what a strong World Series he otherwise had.

Rewind to September 17th, 1991. The Braves were in the midst of a 2-month-long battle with the Los Angeles Dodgers for supremacy in the NL West. Coming from the depths of 3 consecutive last place finishes from 1988-1990, Atlanta was one-half game behind the Dodgers, 82-63 to 83-63.

That day it was announced that Otis Nixon had been suspended for 60 days for violating MLB's drug policy. Nixon was having a career year, with 72 stolen bases and 80 runs scored in only 400 at bats. Nixon was also playing an outstanding center field and was considered the sparkplug of the offense. At the time of Nixon's suspension, he was described by the *New York Times* as "a primary reason the Atlanta Braves are in first place."[1]

In an irony that was lost on no one, Lonnie Smith had had considerable drug problems of his own, also plagued by cocaine addiction, having been compelled to testify in the "Pittsburgh drug trials" in late 1985. Smith and six other players were suspended for a year, but were able to continue playing by agreeing to submit to a number of conditions and undergo regular testing. However, the damage had been done to his reputation and the next two seasons were down ones for Smith, until he was picked up by the Braves in early 1988 and resurrected his career with an excellent 1989 season.

Bobby Cox announced Lonnie Smith would take over as starting left fielder, with Ron Gant moving to center. Smith was hitting .280 at the time, in part-time duty, and was no stranger to high-pressure baseball. Even so, there was concern among fans and media; Nixon had been playing inspired baseball. As it turned out, it's hard to imagine Nixon could have contributed any more to the Braves down the stretch than Lonnie Smith did.

If the Braves themselves were concerned, they certainly didn't show it. On the 18th they defeated the Padres 6-4, exploding for five runs in the top of the first inning. Smith batted leadoff in the game, reaching base four of five plate appearances with two walks and two singles. The next day was a 4-2 10-inning win in which Smith got 3 of Atlanta's 7 hits, scored and drove in two of their four runs, and started the extra-inning rally with a lead-off single.

Over the next six games both Smith and the Braves slipped a bit. Lonnie collected four hits in the six games, scored two, and

A baserunning gaffe by Braves outfielder Lonnie Smith in Game Seven of the 1991 World Series sealed his fate as a goat despite his record-matching home run mark.

drove in two (with one home run), while the Braves dropped four of the six. At the start of play on September 27th, Atlanta faced an uphill climb—two games behind the Dodgers with nine games to go, including the next six on the road.

Longtime Braves fans will remember how amazing the 1991 season was, and that final home stretch was one of the highlights. Atlanta went into the unfriendly confines of the Astrodome, took three straight games, and kept on winning (5 more in-a-row) until they clinched the NL West Crown on the next-to-last day of the season.

In those eight games, Lonnie Smith was one of the standouts. He reached base 15 times in 35 plate appearances, scoring eight runs (at least one in every game but one), and drove in four. Overall, in those final 2 ½ weeks filling in for Otis Nixon, Smith had 16 hits, 8 BB, 2 HBP, and 2 HR, scoring 13 runs and driving in 8. Nothing earth-shattering, but very solid and consistent; in only 3 of the 17 games did he fail to either drive in or score at least one run.

Smith was also no stranger to post-season baseball, having already been a part of 3 World Series winning teams—the 1980 Phillies, the 1982 Cardinals, and the 1985 Royals—one of only a handful of players to play on three winners. In fact, Smith was a major contributor to those three triumphs. In the three clinching games (2 of which were Game Sevens), Lonnie went 5-for-12 with 6 runs scored and 4 RBI.

The Braves won a tough 7-game victory over the favored Pittsburgh Pirates in the NLCS, putting Smith into World Series number four. Bobby Cox was happy to have Smith's experience in the lineup, and he slotted Lonnie in the leadoff spot for in all seven games, either as DH on the road or left field at home.

Smith was quiet the first two games, picking up a walk and run scored in the Game One loss in the Metrodome, and then an 0-for-3 with a sacrifice hit in the 3-2 loss in Game Two. In Game Three he got to work. With the score 2-1 Atlanta in the bottom of the fifth, Smith cranked a solo home run to give the Braves a 3-1 lead, in a game they would hold on to win 5-4 in extra innings. In Game Four he struck again, in an even bigger spot. In the bottom of the 7th inning with 2 out and no one on, Lonnie cranked another solo home run to put the Braves ahead 2-1. The Twins would tie the score in the 8th 2-2 before Atlanta eked out another walkoff win on a sacrifice fly in the bottom of the 9th.

In Game Five the Braves jumped out to a 5-0 lead, but by the 7th the Twins had drawn to 5-3. In the bottom of that inning Smith re-seized the momentum for his team with his third home run in as many games. Ultimately, the final score was 14-5, but at the time Smith went deep, the run was big.

In the three Atlanta victories, Lonnie Smith became only the second player in history to homer in three consecutive games, joining Mr. October himself, Reggie Jackson.

Game Six was another nail-biter, with the Twins ultimately pre-vailing 4-3. Smith chipped in with a walk and a run scored. Which brings us to the fateful Game Seven. In the Game, Smith flied out in the first and struck out in the 10th, and in between reached base 3 times with two singles and a walk. He was the only Braves player to reach base 3 times off the brilliant Jack Morris, and other than David Justice, who had an intentional walk and a single, the only one to reach more than once. Ironically, had Smith made an out leading off the 8th inning rather than knocked a single, he would be remembered as one of the Braves' World Series standouts, rather than be the target of blame.

After Smith's single, Terry Pendleton belted a 1-2 pitch deep to left-center. Smith was running on the pitch and made the mistake of not picking up the hit off of Pendleton's bat. He was then deked by second baseman Chuck Knoblauch who pretended it was a double play ball, though Smith denies that is what made him slow down as he approached the bag. By the time he did pick up the ball, it was too late to try to score.

What is not clear, and what is a question that history has forgotten to ask, is whether or not Smith could have scored on the play or if he even should have tried. The Metrodome was not a big ballpark, Kirby Puckett was a gold glove center fielder with a strong arm, and there were no outs with the 3-4-5 hitters coming up.

What if Smith had gone for home and been thrown out at the plate with no one out? That would have been a far worse outcome than staying at third. In fact, had Smith not been running on the pitch, he would have had to pause near second base to see if the ball would be caught, and may have had no choice but to hold at third given the game situation.

But he did run on the pitch and he did delay on the base paths, so it was up to the meat of the order to try to bring him home. The next batter was Ron Gant, who grounded softly to first base;

with the infield in, the runners had to hold. Gant was followed by David Justice, whom the Twins wisely walked intentionally. Sid Bream then followed with a weak grounder to first, which given Bream's slowness afoot, was turned into an easy 3-2-3 DP. Inning over. Nothing across.

If a target is needed for the finger of failure to point at, Sid Bream is a far more deserving than Lonnie Smith. Smith hit a single in the fateful 8th inning; Bream hit into a double play. In the series, Bream went 3-for-24 with ZERO runs batted in and ZERO runs scored, batting fifth or six in the order. In the World Series the following year he went 3-for-15 for the Braves in their 6-game loss to the Blue Jays, again with zero RBI, though he did manage to cross the plate one time.

The driving force behind Smith becoming the scapegoat of the inning was the commentary of broadcaster Tim McCarver, who at the time made a big deal out of Knoblauch's bluff and the effect it allegedly had on Smith. Numerous replays were shown from numerous angles. The result was a highly critical spotlight shining solely on one of the Braves' outstanding World Series performerss—Lonnie Smith—with his three homers in three consecutive games, all in big situations. Lonnie Smith, whose strong hitting in late September was crucial to the Braves streaking to the division title.

Baseball can be glorious and it can be cruel. Rather than Smith becoming the only player in baseball history to win championships with four different teams, in a series in which he became only the second player in World Series history to homer in three consecutive games, Lonnie Smith now wears the horns of a goat—the guy who cost the Braves the 1991 World Series.

Pummeled Padres

The worst performance by a rotation came courtesy of the 1984 San Diego Padres and it wasn't even close. The Padres' pitching staff was fair to middling during the regular season, finishing fifth in ERA in the National League with a 3.48 mark that was 0.11 better than league average. Eric Show led the team with 15 wins, Mark Thurmond paced the rotation with a 2.97 ERA, and the trio of Goose Gossage, Craig Lefferts, and Dave Dravecky combined to save 43 games and pitched to a collective 2.69 ERA in 364 2/3 innings.

San Diego's World Series rotation—Show, Thurmond, Tim Lollar, and Ed Whitson—pitched to a 3.39 ERA during the season, but started to show their warts in the NLCS against the Cubs with all but Whitson struggling mightily. Show was particularly bad, posting a 13.50 ERA in two starts that comprised only 5 1/3 innings. So it's not all that surprising that the Padres' foursome would have an even tougher time with the more powerful bats of the Detroit Tigers.

But no one expected the mess that helped San Diego to a convincing five-game beat down at the hands of the Motor City Kitties. Game One was actually close as Jack Morris started his World Series resume with a complete game 3-2 victory over Thurmond, who allowed three runs in five innings. It would get worse. Whitson, who allowed only one run in eight innings in his lone start against the Cubs, couldn't make it out of the first inning of Game Two, surrendering three runs on five hits in two-thirds of an inning. Andy Hawkins and Lefferts were brilliant, on the other hand, holding the Tigers to only two hits in 8 1/3 innings for a 5-3 win.

Not to be outdone, Lollar lasted all of an inning and two-thirds in his Game Three

Padres pitcher Eric Show's abysmal 10.13 ERA in the 1984 World Series was actually one of the better marks posted by San Diego starters in that Fall Classic.

start, allowing four runs on four hits, including a homer to Marty Castillo, and four walks. Despite another excellent outing from their bullpen, the Padres lost 5-2. Show had the misfortune of facing Morris in Game Four and he did slightly better than his cohorts, going 2 2/3 innings in a 4-2 loss punctuated by two long balls by Alan Trammell who feasted on Show offerings in the first and third before he was mercifully yanked from the game.

Thurmond was sent to the hill for Game Five and kept the merry-go-round at full speed when he lasted only six batters before being sent to the showers. He allowed five hits to the six men he faced, including a Kirk Gibson homer, and left after having retired one batter. The Padres never recovered and lost, 8-4, the exclamation point supplied by Gibson who smashed a long homer into Tiger Stadium's right field upper deck off Gossage in the eighth for a three-run jolt.

The post-Series autopsy was gruesome. Whitson (40.50), Lollar (21.60), Show (10.13), and Thurmond (10.13) became the only rotation to have four pitchers with ERAs over 10.00 in a single World Series. In fact, no team has ever had more than *two* pitchers post ERAs over 10.00 in a single World Series. The four Padres started five games and threw a total of 10 1/3 innings with Thurmond accounting for more than half.

The Ultimate Fall Classic: Game Seven

October 27, 1991—Atlanta Braves at Minnesota Twins: Comparisons between the 1991 World Series and the 1975 Fall Classic between the Red Sox and Reds were inevitable and appropriate. Four of the first six games were one-run affairs, all having been decided in the winning team's final trip to the plate, including a 12-inning Game Three won by the Braves, 5-4. If anyone could speak to the comparisons it was Twins third baseman and Medford, Massachusetts native Mike Pagliarulo. "I kept thinking of the '75 Series tonight. God, I sound like Pete Rose after that sixth game. But this was the greatest game I ever played in," Pags told the *Boston Globe*'s Dan Shaughnessy after Game Seven.[1] If the '91 Series wasn't the best after six full games, it certainly qualified after the seventh.

What made the 1991 World Series even more compelling was that both teams had risen from last place in their respective divisions only a season before to first place and a league pennant. The feat had never been accomplished before in the long and storied history of the major leagues, then suddenly it was achieved twice in the same season. Either way, someone was about to make history. Tom Kelly, in only his fifth year managing in the bigs, was already in his second World Series after leading the Twins from a record of 74-88 in 1990 to a 95-67 mark and an eight-game advantage over the second-place Chicago White Sox.

Steve Rushin referred to the Twins as "men of the people." Kent Hrbek liked to bowl, Kirby Puckett played pool, and Kevin Tapani worked for Federal Express during the offseason so he'd have something to do during the winter. "Our stars don't seem like stars," Tapani explained. "They're more like...average guys, I guess."[2]

Braves skipper Bobby Cox was in his 10th season, splitting his first eight seasons between Atlanta and Toronto before going back to the Braves halfway through the '90 season. Unlike Kelly, Cox didn't experience immediate success, winning his first division title in his ninth season and his first pennant in his 10th when he guided the Braves from a 65-97 mark in 1990 to a 94-68 record in '91.

Rushin likened the Braves to someone with a dual personality, calling them "alternately captivating and irritating." "This team is somehow, at once, the worst-to-first Cinderella and the wicked stepmother Barbarella,"[3] clearly referring to Braves owner Ted Turner's fiancee, Jane Fonda.

The teams were fairly similar and evenly matched. Atlanta was slightly younger, scored more runs per game relative to league average (4.62/4.10), had a lower ERA (3.49) and was the most defensively efficient team in baseball (.714). The Braves ranked among the top three in all three categories. The Twins scored more runs per game (4.79/4.49) than all but three teams, boasted a better ERA relative to league average (3.69/4.09) and ranked third in the AL in defensive efficiency at .710, and ranked among the top four in all three categories.

Both possessed a solid mixture of veterans and youngsters, although Atlanta had more up-and-coming stars, while Minnesota relied more on older players. The Braves' three best regulars were 31-year-old league MVP Terry Pendleton

(.319/22/86), 25-year-old former Rookie of the Year David Justice (.275/21/87) and 26-year-old 30-30 man Ron Gant (.251/32/105/ 34 SB). Minnesota sported a trio of 31 year olds—DH Chili Davis (.277/29/93), first baseman Kent Hrbek (.284/20/89) and center fielder Kirby Puckett (.319/15/89)—and 27-year-old outfielder Shane Mack (.310/18/74).

The rival pitching staffs were also similarly built, both anchored by a veteran, but led mostly by kids. The Twins were led by 36-year-old grizzled veteran Jack Morris, a 216-game winner with almost 3,300 career innings under his belt. Morris went 18-12 with a 3.43 ERA during the regular season, then beat the Toronto Blue Jays twice in the ALCS. But the staff ace was 23-year-old Scott Erickson who featured a hard sinking fastball on his way to a 20-8 regular season record and a 3.18 ERA. Kevin Tapani, 27, went 16-9 and paced the rotation with a 2.99 ERA, and 29-year-old starter-turned-closer Rick Aguilera pitched to a 2.35 ERA and saved a career-best 42 games.

The Braves also had a veteran in their rotation—34-year-old southpaw Charlie Leibrandt (15-13, 3.49)—and bullpen—36-year-old closer Juan Berenguer (2.24, 17 saves) and 32-year-old closer Alejandro Pena (1.40, 11 saves)—but most of the staff was made up of twenty-somethings, like 25-year-old ace Tom Glavine (20-11, 2.55), 21-year-old Steve Avery (18-8, 3.38), 24-year-old John Smoltz (14-13, 3.80), 23-year-old Kent Mercker (2.58, 6 saves) and 24-year-old Mike Stanton (2.88, 7 saves).

Avery and Smoltz really came into their own against the Pirates in the NLCS, going a combined 4-0 with a 0.85 ERA in their four starts, and the staff as a whole allowed only 11 earned runs in seven games. The Twins' pitching wasn't as good against Toronto, pitching to a 3.33 ERA, but they plated 27 runs in five games and scored almost twice as many per contest as the Braves, who recorded an anemic average of 2.71.

Heading into the World Series it looked like it would be a match-up between the Braves' hot, young arms and the Twins' hot, veteran bats. The latter took Game One, 5-2, behind Morris, then the Twins took the second game despite a four-hitter by Glavine, who surrendered only one earned run through eight but was victimized by a David Justice first-inning error that Chili Davis capitalized on by belting a two-out, two-run homer three batters later. Tapani was equally effective, allowing only two runs through eighth innings, and kept his team in the game long enough for them to score the winning run in the bottom of the eighth for a 3-2 win.

The Series shifted to Atlanta where the Braves took the next three to move to within a win of their first title since 1957 when they were still in Milwaukee. Game Three was a see-saw affair that went into the 12th inning knotted at 4-4 before Mark Lemke drove in Justice with the winning run in the bottom of the frame. Game Four was also decided by one run and came down to the Braves' final at-bat in which pinch hitter Jerry Willard knocked in Lemke with a sacrifice fly to tie the Series at two wins apiece with the 3-2 victory. The Braves took the Twins out behind the woodshed in Game Five and pasted them by a 14-5 count, but Minnesota came back with a thrilling 11-inning win in Game Six in which Kirby Puckett belted a lead-off homer off Charlie Leibrandt in the bottom of the 11th to give the Twins a 4-3 victory and send the Series to a seventh game.

Game Seven pitted Morris against Smoltz, a rematch of Game Four in which both hurlers threw well but earned no-decisions. Morris went into the seventh game of the '91 Series with a post-season record of 6-1 and an ERA of 3.03, and had already copped a title in 1984 with the Detroit Tigers. Smoltz, a Michigan native, was a 17-year-old Tiger fan in 1984, who was drafted in 1985 by the team he grew up rooting for, but was traded to Atlanta in 1987 for veteran hurler Doyle Alexander. Now the boy was a man and was going up against his boyhood idol and one of the toughest competitors in baseball in a winner-take-all battle. Smoltz had already acclimated himself nicely to the postseason, having gone 2-0 with a 2.02 ERA, so this promised to be an epic duel.

The pitchers exchanged perfect innings in the first before Justice reached Morris for a lead-off single in the second. Morris retired the next three Braves, then Smoltz ran into a little trouble when he surrendered back-to-back two-out singles to Brian Harper and Shane Mack before escaping the inning. Atlanta threatened in the third when Rafael Belliard singled with one out and advanced to second on a passed ball, and Lonnie Smith walked, but Morris retired Pendleton and Gant, and the game went into the bottom of the third with no score.

And so it went.

Smoltz allowed a one-out double to Dan Gladden, who reached third on a deep liner to right, but the Braves hurler fanned Puckett to strand the go-ahead run. Morris surrendered a two-out double to Brian Hunter in the fourth but coaxed catcher Greg Olson to line out to right to end the mini threat; Smoltz hit Kent Hrbek in the hand with a pitch to lead off the bottom of the fourth, but set down Chili Davis, Harper and Mack on harmless fly balls and pop-ups. The Braves threatened again in the top of the fifth when Lemke led off with a single, moved to second on a Belliard sacrifice, then advanced to third on a bunt single by Smith, who dived into the first base bag just ahead of the throw. But Morris buckled down again, popped up Pendleton and struck out Gant to get out of the jam.

Then both pitchers got stubborn. Smoltz allowed a two-out single to Gladden in the bottom of the fifth, then retired the next seven straight. Morris retired six in a row before giving up a lead-off single to Smith in the top of the eighth. That's when things began to get interesting. Pendleton smoked a shot to left-center field during a delayed steal and the speedy Smith, who'd stolen more than 350 bases in his career at that point, should have scored easily from first base.

But an amazing thing happened on the way to home plate; Smith lost sight of the ball halfway between first and second and was deked by second baseman Chuck Knoblauch and shortstop Greg Gagne, who pretended to turn a double play. By the time Smith realized the ball was banging off the outfield wall, he only had time enough to advance to third. "If you're scoring, the play that probably decided the 1991 World Series goes Knoblauch-to-Gagne-to-Nobody, the greatest double play never made," wrote Thomas Boswell. "Lonnie Smith still wonders where the ball is. He hasn't seen it yet. He's still watching Chuck Knoblauch and Greg Gagne pretend to turn a phantom double play—a mime, a joke, a sucker play, a moment of genius..."[4]

Instead of a run in and a man on third with Gant coming up, the Braves had runners at second and third with no outs. Gant grounded weakly to first and couldn't get the run home. Tom Kelly ordered an intentional walk to Justice, bringing Sid Bream to the plate with the bases loaded. Bream was 3-for-23 in the World Series at that point and 0-for-5 with runners in scoring position. The Twins turned a real double play this time, first-to-home-and-back-to-first, to get out of the inning and the Metrodome crowd erupted into a frenzy. It turned out to be the Braves' last opportunity to score.

It looked like the Twins were going to break the scoreless tie in the bottom of the eighth when pinch hitter Randy Bush singled and pinch runner Al Newman advanced to third on a one-out hit-and-run single by Knoblauch to put runners at first and third with only one away. Cox removed Smoltz from the game in favor of lefty Mike Stanton, who held left-handed batters to a .194 average during the season and allowed only one homer to a lefty all year. Cox had Stanton walk Puckett to load the bases for port-side swinging slugger Kent Hrbek, and the move paid off when Hrbek hit a looper to Lemke, who stepped on second for an inning-ending twin killing.

Morris settled down again and retired the side in the top of the ninth on only eight pitches, bringing the Metrodome crowd to its feet when he had two strikes on Lemke and was one strike away from his ninth shutout inning. When Kelly told Morris he was through for the night, the hurler insisted he stay in and finish what he started. "Who was going to take him out of this game?" Randy Bush asked later. "If it was T.K., Jack would have punched him, kicked him—he might have killed him. He wasn't coming out."[5] Kelly concurred. When asked what it would have taken to get Morris out of the game, the Twins skipper smiled and replied, "Probably a shotgun."[6]

When the Twins rallied in the bottom of the ninth it looked like Morris wouldn't have to pitch the "112 innings" he insisted he could go if the game continued. Chili Davis led off the inning with a long single that was played well by Justice and was replaced by pinch runner Jarvis Brown. Harper laid down a bunt between Stanton and Bream that went for a hit and put runners on first and second with nobody out. Stanton injured himself on the play, pulling a muscle in his back, and Alejandro Pena entered the game to face Mack, Pagliarulo, and pinch hitter Paul Sorrento. The Braves reliever escaped the jam when Mack grounded into a double play and Sorrento whiffed after an intentional pass to Pags, sending the game into extra frames.

Like a proud gunfighter, Morris strode to the mound and dispatched his enemies without so much as breaking a sweat, setting down pinch hitter Jeff Blauser on a pop to Harper, fanning Smith, and coaxing Pendleton to ground out to short. That set up the climactic ending of only the second World Series Game Seven to end 1-0.

Gladden smacked a broken-bat double to left to lead off the bottom of the 10th, then advanced to third on a Knoblauch sacrifice bunt. Cox had little choice but to intentionally walk Puckett and Hrbek to load the sacks and set up a force at home.

Cox pulled his outfielders in so they'd have a chance to get Gladden at the plate on a shallow fly ball. Kelly called upon 29-year-old switch-hitter Gene Larkin to pinch hit for Jarvis Brown. Larkin hit a career-best .286 in 1991 and reached base at a .361 clip, but had little power, slugging only .373, and was battling tendinitis in his knee that held him to only three plate appearances in the ALCS and three in the World Series. When he stepped into the box with the bases loaded and one out in the bottom of the 10th, it was Larkin's fourth and most important trip to the dish. "You can taste the pressure here in the dome as Alejandro straightens up," announced Vin Scully.

"The noisy home crowd of 55,000 was on its feet and creating a snowstorm by waving its white homer hankies," wrote Ira Berkow of the New York Times. "And Larkin responded."[7] Larkin wasted no time, swinging at Pena's first pitch and punching it into left-center field where it fell in for the game-winning hit. The Twins were champions by the slimmest of margins after an epic 1-0 victory.

Berkow called Game Seven of the '91 Fall Classic "a gift from above" and claimed that it was the best sporting event anyone had ever witnessed. "Nothing was happening," he wrote about the final game between the Twins and Braves, "nothing, nothing, nothing, nothing but tension...It appeared that the best and concluding moments of this baseball season—maybe the best of any season—might last forever."[8]

Morris was named Series MVP. "I don't know where the strength came from," he said after the game. "My arm was alive. I felt real strong, I don't know how or why. Pitching two games on three days' rest, this isn't supposed to happen. The baseball gods in the sky must have blessed me tonight."[9]

They blessed us all, Jack.

Source Notes

PART I

Have We Met? The Unlikeliest World Series Heroes   p3

1. The Boston National League team had been known as the Red Stockings, (1876-1882), Beaneaters (1883-1906), Doves (1907-1910), and Rustlers (1911) before becoming the Braves in 1912.
2. *Chicago Tribune*, October 6, 1914
3. *Boston Globe*, October 11, 1926
4. *Washington Post*, April 6, 1969; Statistics don't appear to back up the claim that Duncan was a superior defensive catcher, and Bill James gave him a grade of D+ in his book *Win Shares*.

Ed Doheny: The Paranoid Pirate   p15

1. http://sabr.org/bioproj/person/023bfd7e
2. Boston Globe, October 12, 1903
3. Ibid.

The Ultimate Fall Classic: Game One   p18

1. *Washington Post*, October 15, 1988
2. Ibid.
3. *Orlando Sentinel*, March 5, 1988
4. Ibid.
5. *Philadelphia Inquirer*, October 16, 1988
6. *Philadelphia Inquirer*, October 16, 1988
7. *Boston Globe*, October 16, 1988
8. *Los Angeles Times*, October 16, 1988
9. *Boston Globe*, October 17, 1988
10. Ibid.

Bill Abstein: Floundering at First Base   p27

1. Boston Globe, January 27, 1909. Pittsburgh was spelled "Pittsburg" until 1911.
2. St. Louis Post-Dispatch, February 3, 1910
3. New York Times, November 19, 1909
4. St. Louis Post-Dispatch, February 3, 1910
5. http://baseballhistorydaily.com/2013/02/20/bill-abstein-denies-he-is-a-bonehead
6. St. Louis Post-Dispatch, October 16, 1909
7. Washington Post, October 15, 1909
8. St. Louis Post-Dispatch, October 16, 1909
9. Ibid.
10. Ibid.
11. http://baseballhistorydaily.com/2013/02/20/bill-abstein-denies-he-is-a-bonehead
12. New York Times, November 19, 1909.

Hello, Goodbye: Reb Russell's "Perfect" Game   p32

1. *Hartford Courant*, October 13, 1917
2. Ibid.
3. *Chicago Tribune*, March 27, 1917
4. *Los Angeles Times*, October 13, 1917
5. *Chicago Tribune*, October 13, 1917
6. *New York Times*, October 13, 1917
7. *Chicago Tribune*, October 13, 1917

The Ultimate Fall Classic: Game Two   p36

1. *Boston Globe*, October 3, 1916
2. *Boston Globe*, October 3, 1916
3. *New York Times*, October 9, 1916
4. Bill James and Rob Neyer, *The Neyer/James Guide to Pitchers: An Historical Compendium of Pitching, Pitchers, and Pitches* (New York, New York: Simon & Schuster, Inc., 2004), p. 388
5. *Boston Globe*, October 10, 1916
6. Ibid.
7. *Chicago Tribune*, October 10, 1916
8. *Atlanta Constitution*, October 10, 1916
9. *Boston Globe*, October 10, 1916
10. Ibid.
11. Ibid.
12. *Boston Globe*, October 10, 1916
13. Glenn Stout and Richard A. Johnson, *Red Sox Century* (Boston: Houghton Mifflin, 2000), p. 111

1920: A True Fall Classic   p45

1. *Boston Globe*, September 23, 1920
2. *Boston Globe*, September 24, 1920; Harold Seymour, *Baseball: The Golden Age* (New York: Oxford University Press, 1971), p. 298
3. *Boston Globe*, October 4, 1920
4. First baseman Chick Gandil was also part of the scandal and may have been the ring leader, but he retired before the 1920 season and was no longer active.
5. Mike Sowell, *The Pitch That Killed* (Chicago: Ivan R. Dee, 1989), p. 267
6. *Boston Globe*, October 5, 1920; Doc was actually born on September 9, 1887 in Cleveland, Tennessee while Jimmy was born on December 10, 1889 in Cleveland, Tennessee., and was more than two years younger.
7. *Boston Globe*, October 11, 1920
8. *New York Times*, October 11, 1920
9. Ibid.
10. Cleveland shortstop Neal Ball was credited with an unassisted triple play on July 19, 1909, but Paul Hines may or may not have turned the trick on May 8, 1878.

Scalped by More Than the Indians   p51

1. St. Louis Post-Dispatch, October 9, 1920
2. New York Times, October 10, 1920
3. Boston Globe, October 10, 1920
4. Boston Globe, October 12, 1920
5. http://sabr.org/bioproj/person/566fa007
6. New York Times, October 13, 1920
7. Ibid.
8. Ibid.
9. St. Louis Post-Dispatch, October 15, 1920

Jesse Haines Out-Babes "The Babe"   p54

1. Boston Globe, October 6, 1926
2. New York Times, October 6, 1926
3. Boston Globe, October 6, 1926

The Ultimate Fall Classic: Game Three   p57

1. *Chicago Tribune*, October 3, 1919
2. Eliot Asinof, *Eight Men Out* (New York, New York: Pocket Books, 1963), pp. 108-109
3. *Chicago Tribune*, October 4, 1919
4. *New York Tribune*, October 4, 1919
5. Ibid.

6. Ibid.

7. Ibid.

8. William A. Cook, *The 1919 World Series: What Really Happened?* (Jefferson, North Carolina: McFarland & Company, Inc., Publishers, 2001), p. 39

9. *New York Times*, October 4, 1919

10. *New York Tribune*, October 4, 1919

11. *Boston Globe*, October 4, 1919

12. Ibid.

13. *New York Times*, October 4, 1919

14. Ibid.

15. *New York Tribune*, October 4, 1919

16. *Boston Globe*, October 4, 1919

PART 2

MVP-lease! The Biggest World Series Flops   p69

No source notes

Welcome to the Bigs, Meat   p74

1. *Chicago Tribune*, October 8, 1939

2. *Boston Globe*, October 8, 1939. Gomez was going for his seventh straight World Series win against no losses.

3. *Hartford Courant*, October 8, 1939

Brother Can You Spare a Win?   p76

1. *Washington Post*, August 6, 1940

The Ultimate Fall Classic: Game Four   p79

1. *New York Times*, October 13, 1929

2. Ibid.

3. Ibid.

4. Ibid.

5. *Washington Post*, October 13, 1929

6. *Chicago Tribune*, October 13, 1929

7. *New York Times*, October 13, 1929

8. Bill James and Rob Neyer, *The Neyer/James Guide to Pitchers: An Historical Compendium of Pitching, Pitchers, and Pitches* (New York: Simon & Schuster, 2004), p. 290

9. *Washington Post*, October 13, 1929

10. Roberts Ehrgott, *Mr. Wrigley's Ballclub: Chicago and the Cubs During the Jazz Age* (Lincoln: University of Nebraska Press, 2013), p. 201

11. Ibid.

A Returning Vet's Unusual At Bat   p88

No source notes

Hitless Wonders: An All-Time 0-fer Lineup   p90

1. Peter Golenbock, *Bums: An Oral History of the Brooklyn Dodgers* (Mineola, New York: Dover Publications, 2010), p. 345

Mickey Grasso: POW at the Plate   p95

1. Much of this piece comes from Cort Vitty's article in *The National Pastime*. Cort Vitty: "Mickey Grasso: the Catcher Was a POW," in Bob Brown, ed.: *Monumental Baseball: The National Pastime in the National Capital Region, The National Pastime*, SABR, Number 39, 2009, pp. 81-83.

Here's Your Hat...What's Your Hurry   p97

1. Bill Stafford had a better ERA at 2.25, but didn't make his debut until August 17 and started only eight games.
2. Rob Neyer, *Rob Neyer's Big Book of Baseball Blunders: A Complete Guide to the Worst Decisions and Stupidest Moments in Baseball History*, (New York: Touchstone, 2006), pp. 97-98
3. Ibid., p. 98
4. *Hartford Courant*, October 4, 1960
5. Neyer, *Big Book of Baseball Blunders*, p. 96
6. Video of the play shows Virdon taking off with the pitch, making it look like a straight steal.
7. *Boston Globe*, October 6, 1960
8. Ibid.
9. Ibid.
10. *Los Angeles Times*, October 6, 1960
11. *Los Angeles Times*, October 6, 1960
12. *Boston Globe*, October 6, 1960
13. *Hartford Courant*, October 6, 1960
14. *Hartford Courant*, October 10, 1960
15. *New York Times*, October 11, 1960
16. *Chicago Tribune*, October 11, 1960
17. *Christian Science Monitor*, October 11, 1960
18. *New York Times*, October 11, 1960
19. *Hartford Courant*, October 11, 1960
20. Ibid.

The Ultimate Fall Classic: Game Five   p103

1. Don Larsen, *The Perfect Yankee: The Incredible Story of the Greatest Miracle in Baseball History* (Urbana, Illinois: Sagamore Publishing, 1996), Introduction
2. *Washington Post*, October 5, 1956
3. *Los Angeles Times*, September 25, 1994
4. *Chicago Defender*, October 9, 1956
5. *Chicago Tribune*, October 9, 1956
6. *Chicago Defender*, October 9, 1956
7. *New York Times*, October 9, 1956
8. *Hartford Courant*, October 9, 1956
9. *New York Times*, October 9, 1956
10. *Sports Illustrated*, October 14, 1996
11. Ibid.
12. *New York Times*, October 9, 1956
13. *Chicago Defender*, October 9, 1956
14. *New York Times*, October 9, 1956
15. *Washington Post*, October 9, 1956
16. *New York Times*, October 9, 1956
17. Ibid.
18. *Chicago Defender*, October 9, 1956
19. *New York Times*, October 9, 1956
20. *Chicago Defender*, October 9, 1956
21. *New York Times*, October 9, 1956
22. *Chicago Defender*, October 9, 1956
23. *Chicago Tribune*, October 9, 1956
24. Ibid.
25. Ibid.
26. *New York Times*, October 9, 1956
27. Ibid.
28. Ibid.

PART III

Mind-Numbing Numbers: The Oddest World Series Stat Lines   p115

1. WHIP stands for (Walks + Hits)/Innings Pitched.
2. The worst BB/9IP ratio belongs to Scott Kazmir who walked 10 batters in 10 innings for the Tampa Bay Rays in the 2008 World Series.

He Ain't Heavy...He's a Boyer   p122

1. Bill James, *The New Bill James Historical Baseball Abstract* (New York: Free Press, 2001), p. 262
2. Bill James, *Win Shares* (Morton Grove, Illinois: STATS, Inc., 2002), p. 144

The Mickey Lolich Miracle   p125

1. *Boston Globe*, October 4, 1968
2. Ibid.
3. As of this writing, Joe Blanton has also homered in a World Series—Game Four, 2008—but not in a regular season game. He's still active.
4. *Boston Globe*, October 4, 1968
5. Ibid.

Protest Flags, Vietnam, and the 1969 Mets   p129

1. *Boston Globe*, July 1, 1969
2. Ibid.
3. Ibid.
4. Ibid.
5. *New York Times*, September 28, 1969
6. Ibid.
7. *New York Times*, October 15, 1969
8. Ibid.
9. Ibid.
10. *Chicago Tribune*, October 16, 1969
11. *New York Times*, October 16, 1969
12. Ibid.
13. *Washington Post*, October 16, 1969
14. Ibid.
15. Ibid.

Ultimate Fall Classic: Game Six   p132

1. *South Florida Sun-Sentinel*, July 23, 1989
2. *Boston Globe*, April 1, 2010

Jim Palmer Walks Like a Man   p141

1. Cincinnati's Glenn Braggs drove in two runs with two groundouts in four at-bats in the 1990 World Series, but failed to record a hit in four at-bats. Tampa Bay's Gabe Gross drove in two runs in Game Three of the 2008 World Series on a second inning sacrifice fly and a seventh inning groundout, but went 0 for 3 in the Series and became the third player to drive in two runs in a World Series without getting a hit.

Bruce Kison Comes to Earth   p144

1. *Boston Globe*, October 11, 1979

Lonnie Smith: Braves' Hero   p148

1. *New York Times,* September 17, 1991

Pummeled Padres   p154

No source notes

Ultimate Fall Classic: Game Seven   p157

1. *Boston Globe*, October 29, 1991
2. *Sports Illustrated*, October 28, 1991
3. Ibid.
4. *Washington Post*, October 28, 1991
5. *Sports Illustrated*, November 4, 1991
6. *New York Times*, October 28, 1991
7. *New York Times*, October 28, 1991
8. *New York Times*, October 29, 1991
9. *Sports Illustrated*, October 28, 1991